This book is dedicated to my wife Yoshiko
and to my two sons, Tarō and Jirō

HISTORICAL NARA

With illustrations and guide maps

By HERBERT E. PLUTSCHOW

The **Japan Times**, Ltd.

ISBN4-7890-0226-8

First edition: November 1983

Illustrations by courtesy of Kyoto University Library
Photos by The Japan Times, Michio Noguchi, Kintetsu, Otsuka
Kogeisha
Guide maps by White Sheet
Jacket design by Koji Detake

Published by The Japan Times, Ltd.
5-4, Shibaura 4-chome, Minato-ku, Tokyo 108, Japan

Printed in Japan

ACKNOWLEDGEMENTS

A number of people have helped me in the writing of this book: Gaudenz
Domenig, a Swiss specialist on Japanese Shintō, has opened my eyes to archaic
Shintō in its relations to time and space, deities and men; Kenzaburō Torigoe,
whose *Tennō-ken no Kigen* (1976) and *Kamigami to Tennō no aida* (1970) convinced me of the dual emperorship in the early Yamato Period; and Margaret
Robe and Allison Rew who improved my style and this project with
numerous suggestions. Many thanks too to Dr. and Mrs. Uchimura of
Kushira, Kagoshima Prefecture under whose warm hospitality I wrote portions of this book.

CONTENTS

vi

Illustrations (All by courtesy of Kyoto University Library)
Saikoku Meisho-zue. Yamato no Kuni, Vols. 7-10, Edo, Kyoto, Osaka, 1853.
Yamato Meisho-zue. In 7 Vols., Kyoto, 1791.

SHINTŌ AND THE RISE OF THE EMPERORS

Just as the city of Rome was not built in a day, neither was the city of Nara. In fact one has to delve back some three or four hundred years prior to its founding to trace the roots of this early Japanese capital, for the story of Nara is, by and large, the history of ancient Japan. It is also the history of the Yamato (or Nara) Plain, where it is located, and where, from about the fourth century on, much of Japanese civilization as we know it today evolved. For this reason, a study of Nara demands consideration of the political and religious tumult and cultural transformation of those centuries that ultimately resulted in the founding of Nara as capital of Japan in the year 708. In a sense, the Yamato Plain and Nara are the very essence of Japan, and wherever one might be within their boundaries one stands unmistakably on the pages of ancient history.

THE YAMATO (NARA) PLAIN

"Oh, what a beautiful country we have become possessed of!"
Emperor Jimmu

Tradition has it that in the year 667 B.C. Jimmu, a descendant of the mythical ancestors of the imperial line, set out from Kyūshū and skirting the Inland Sea travelled northwards, intending to conquer the Yamato Plain, which he believed to be the center of the world. Local tribes repulsed his first attack from the west but a second assault proved more successful. The sun goddess, Jimmu's great-great-grandmother, guided him through the southern mountains of Kumano and Yoshino so that by attacking from the south he was able to subdue the tribes of the Yamato Plain becoming Japan's first recorded emperor. Jimmu's successors were to reside in this plain or its

2

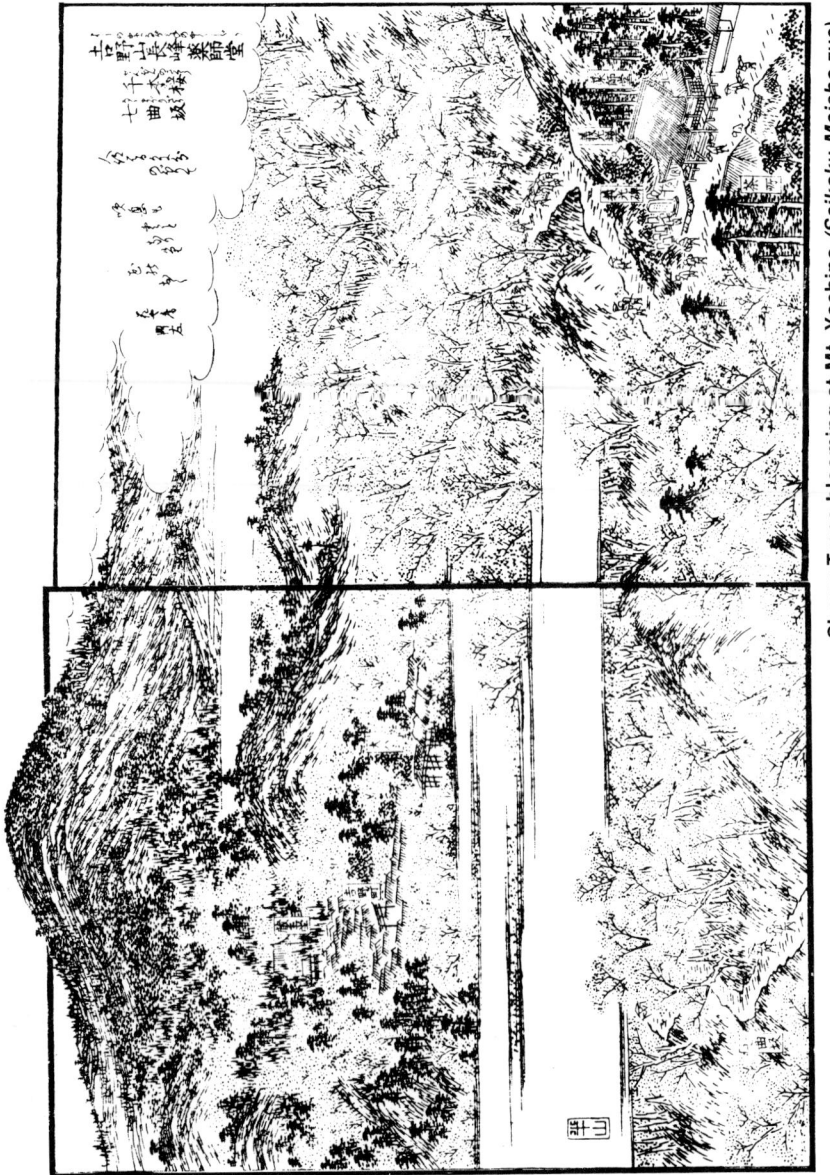

Cherry Trees blooming at Mt. Yoshino (*Saikoku Meisho-zue*)

immediate vicinity as sovereigns of the nation until the 19th century; hence Yamato and Japan are often regarded as one and the same.

The Yamato Plain is relatively small: approximately thirty kilometers from north to south and fifteen kilometers from east to west. What made this plain so desirable for the early emperors of Japan was not its size so much as its geographical setting. Protected in the north by the mountains of Tamba and Hira, in the east by Kasagi, in the west by Kongō, Katsuragi and Ikoma, and in the south by the hills of Takami and Yoshino, the Yamato Plain was easily defendable and afforded fairly good communication with the rest of Japan through low passes and rivers. The plain's central location in Honshū, Japan's main island, proved a good starting point for the conquest of the rest of Japan. Because Japan's native religion, Shintō (literally, 'The Way of Gods'), projects spiritual attributes onto the landscape, the Yamato Plain received its religious geography from an early date. Some of the surrounding mountains were believed to be the abode of the dead: in particular, Katsuragi, Nijō and the mountains of Hase. Most mountains were also revered as the dwelling places of local deities: Mt. Miwa, Yoshino and the Three Mountains of Yamato, for example. Into these mountains only initiated priests and emperors entered, and only after performing thorough purification rites. It was from the local deities native to the mountains that the emperors and priests were believed to attain the powers to rule, prophesy, exorcise and heal.

These sacred mountains, which provided a shield and protection from the outer world, symbolized to the ancient Japanese the eternity and immutability of all things; yet they were at the same time regarded as the source of change that was brought down out of the mountains by the rivers and winds. Spring came down from the Yoshino mountains with the Yoshino River, and storms blowing along the Tatsuta River from the west were thought to bring autumn. (Even today Yoshino is associated with spring mists and cherry blossoms and Tatsuta, the dwelling of the storm deity, with

4

Asuka River *(Saikoku Meisho-zue)*

crimson leaves.) The Asuka River with its changing currents was less a symbol of seasonal mutability than of the evanescence and frailty of all human existence.

The first emperors and their religious and secular functions: Many scholars dispute the traditional date given for Jimmu's conquest of the Yamato Plain. Most believe it took place in the third or fourth century A.D., considerably later than the legendary year of 667 B.C. Some historians doubt even the very existence of Jimmu who, they claim, was a creation of the eighth century Japanese historians' attempt to approximate Japan's early history with that of China. According to the findings of Kenzaburō Torigoe, a specialist in early Japanese history, Jimmu did in fact conquer a portion of the Yamato Plain and established the Katsuragi Dynasty, so named because Jimmu and the succeeding eight emperors lived and were buried to the east of Mt. Katsuragi in the area of present-day Gose City. The tenth emperor* of the Yamato Plain, who like Jimmu is also referred to in the histories as "Emperor who first ruled the Land," settled near Mt. Miwa in the central region of the plain. It was from here that the early emperors gradually brought under their control the rest of the Yamato Plain as well as the country stretching from Kyūshū northwards to present-day Tokyo.

The early emperors were an ungracious lot. During a banquet held in his honor by a local chieftain, Jimmu is said to have slain his host; and Jimmu's two sons from his second marriage apparently murdered their half-brother from his first marriage, generating the often bloody successional disputes that were to plague the imperial family and early Japanese history until the eighth century.

Torigoe's research also reveals that from the reign of Jimmu's successor until that of the fourteenth emperor, imperial power was divided between two brothers; the elder was responsible for performing the religious, ritual functions and the younger for executing

---

* The dates of these early emperors are not known.

Emperor Jimmu's Tomb *(Saikoku Meisho-zue)*

the political functions at the direction of his elder brother. This is illustrated in the Chinese *History of the Sui Dynasty* (c. 630) in which a Japanese envoy to the Sui court, asked by the Chinese emperor as to the manner in which the Japanese sovereigns ruled the country, is recorded as replying: "The King of Wa [Japan] deems heaven to be his elder brother and the sun, his younger. Before break of dawn he attends the court, and, sitting cross-legged, listens to appeals. Just as soon as the sun rises, he ceases these duties, saying that he hands them over to his brother." The ritual functions were conducted by a nocturnal emperor-priest and the secular aspects of rule by his subordinate servant, the diurnal secular emperor respectively.

Ritual purity being essential at all times, the priest-emperor was not allowed to take a wife and had, therefore, no offspring. Thus it was from the children of the younger brother, the secular-emperor as one might call him, that the succeeding dual rulers were descended. Nevertheless, since it was an age in which religion preceded politics in priority, the priest-emperors were more powerful and held in greater esteem than their secular counterparts. It is interesting though that early Japanese histories such as the *Kojiki* (Record of Ancient Matters) of 712 and the *Nihon Shoki* (Annals of Japan) of 720 make no reference to the priest-emperors. These histories were compiled according to Chinese principles of historiography, and in keeping with the notion of Chinese emperorship in which one monarch combined both functions, only the secular emperor is listed as sole ruler. All early secular emperors did, however, have elder priestly brothers and in spite of the difficulties in identifying tombs, there is at least one indication that the tomb of the twelfth emperor's elder brother, ignored in the histories, is larger than that of his younger brother who is named as emperor in the *Kojiki* and the *Nihon Shoki*.

This division of Japanese imperial rule into religious and secular functions is further recorded in the *History of the Wei Dynasty* (220-265) in the description of a yet unidentified Japanese priestess-queen who ruled over an also equally unidentified area of Japan.

The country formerly had a man as ruler. For some
seventy or eighty years after that there were disturbances and
warfare. Thereupon the people agreed upon a woman for their
ruler. Her name was Pimiko. She occupied herself with magic
and sorcery, bewitching the people. Though mature in age,
she remained unmarried. She had a younger brother who
assisted her in ruling the country. After she became the ruler,
there were few who saw her. She had one thousand women as
attendants, but only one man. He served her food and drink
and acted as a medium of communication. She resided in a
palace surrounded by towers and stockades, with armed
guards in a state of constant vigilance . . .

(*Sources of Japanese Tradition.* Vol. 1, pp. 5-6)

Such shamanistic empresses, dominant in early Japan, probably ruled
over a federacy of local clans and account for the matrilineal system in
existence in Japanese society until the Heian Period (795-1185) when it
was gradually replaced by a patrilineal system.

Imperial rituals: Sento (Transfer of the Capital): In order to better
understand the separation of imperial rule into religious and political
spheres, it is worthwhile examining some of the religious functions of
the early emperors. Though most sources concern later emperors who
executed both functions, the descriptions of imperial rituals give a
fairly accurate picture of their significance and how they were
performed.

An important rite which all emperors faithfully observed until the
reign of Empress Jitō (r. 686-697) was the renewal or rebuilding of
imperial palaces. Shintō emphasized ritual purity and required that the
site of an imperial palace, and consequently the entire capital, be
abandoned if it became ritually unclean. Impurity resulted from illness,
death, assassination, natural calamities such as flooding and epidemics
and political disturbances. When an emperor died, for instance, his

successor would transfer the capital in order to be enthroned in an unpolluted, ritually clean environment. (As a rule, these palaces, like many of the Shintō shrines, were simple structures and were easily built elsewhere with a limited amount of labor and effort.)

Imperial rituals: Daijō-e (Great Feast of Kingship):   Every geographically and topographically distinct territory was believed to be the domain of a local deity. When usurped of parts of their territory for purposes such as settling, cultivation or the erection of imperial palaces, these local divinities would vent their wrath by perpetrating floods or other natural disasters. In order to placate the deities, the emperors had to observe several rituals that were a combination of politics and magic. Neglect of the rituals resulted in the emperors' inability to impose authority over a territory, or to control the populace and preserve the peace and harmony in their realm.

    After ascending the throne, an emperor would observe Daijō-e, or the Great Feast of Kingship, a ritual upon which much of his imperial potency depended. To represent the nation at this ritual, one eastern province and one western province were selected by divination. Two very simple hut-like structures, one for each province, were erected and fruit and rice indigenous to each of the provinces displayed inside. The emperor then proceeded to each building at night and partook of the produce, all of which had been grown in particularly sacred fields. In poems read to the emperor by virgin maidens representing the provinces' powerful local shrines, the names of their enshrined deities were revealed. The ancient Japanese believed that the power of something resided in a word or sound — a concept known as Kotodama (Word Soul) — and that revelation of the name or sound was a magical means to assume control over it. In the eating of fruit indigenous to the two provinces selected to represent the nation and in the speaking of the names of their most powerful provincial deities the emperor was magically imbued with the power of the divinities as they submitted themselves to imperial rule.

Emperor Jimmu's Kuni-mi (Looking Down Over the Land) Ritual *(Saikoku Meisho-zue)*

Throughout the ceremony the emperor wore a white dress which has been explained as symbolizing his loss of self, for an emperor could not receive the soul of the nation without first giving up his own. Another interpretation sees in this ritual a marriage of heaven, represented by the emperor's white dress, and earth necessary to ensure the earth's fertility. As such it was also an important source of imperial charisma, for in a basically agrarian society fertility was believed to rest upon an interaction of heaven, represented by the emperor, and earth, represented by the local deities. It therefore comes as no surprise that both the emperors and some of the local clans claimed descent from the sun as it was the sun in heaven which nurtured and ensured the growth of living things.

Imperial rituals: Kuni-mi (Looking Down Over the Land): Another important ancient ordinance upon which the political charisma of the emperors no less depended was the *kuni-mi*, or "looking down over the land," for which the emperors would climb sacred mountains in order to survey their realm from a high vantage point. By doing so, the emperors were permeated with power since looking down upon something was thought to be an effective means to possess and control it. Where there were no hills, special platforms were erected instead. The same ritual was regularly performed by farmers who would climb hills or even trees overlooking their fields.

The first recorded *kuni-mi* was carried out by Emperor Jimmu upon Mt. Hohoma (also Hotsuma, near present Gose City).

> The palanquin made a circuit in the course of which the Emperor ascended the Hill Waki Kamu no Hotsuma. Here, having viewed the shape of the land on all sides, he said: — "Oh! What a beautiful country we have become possessed of! Though a blessed land of inner-tree-fibre, yet it resembles a dragon-fly licking its hinder-parts." From this it first received the name of Akitsu-shima.
>
> *Nihon Shoki* (Translated by W.G. Aston)

Bestowing a name upon a territory was another magical means to pacify a local deity prior to occupying its territory. The use of the word "Akitsu," meaning "dragonfly," as a metaphor of the territory Jimmu was looking out upon, reveals also an agricultural purpose to the ritual since dragonflies were thought to eat insects harmful to the crops.

To accompany the *kuni-mi* ritual, *kuni-home*, or "poems in praise of the land," were often composed as yet another mystical device by which to impose imperial authority over the land. Emperor Ōjin, the fifteenth emperor after Jimmu, composed the following *kuni-home* poem:

> Looking over Katsuno
> Of the thousand leaves
> I see enough food growing
> In the orchards —
> I see my country is well.
>
> *(Nihon Shoki)*

The following typical example is recorded in the *Manyōshū* (a collection of poems dating from the mid-eighth century). It was composed either by Emperor Jomei (r. 628-641), the thirty-first emperor, or more likely by a member of his entourage:

> *Climbing Mt. Kagu and Looking Upon the Land*
>
> Countless are the mountains in Yamato,
> But perfect is the heavenly hill of Kagu;
> When I climb it and survey my realm,
> Over the wide plain the smoke-wreaths rise and rise,
> Over the wide lake the gulls are on the wing;
> A beautiful land it is, the Land of Yamato.

Praising the land in poems was another form of Word Soul intended to placate the local deities robbed of their territories.

Imperial rituals: Kamikakari (Divining the Ancestral Will): An emperor further needed to be able to enter into communication with the ancestors of the imperial family. Jimmu's success in conquering the Yamato Plain was attributed to his ability to communicate with his great-great-grandmother, the sun goddess. Although the following dates from a time when the religious and secular duality of rule was coming to an end (and so we find a priestess-empress married to the secular emperor), it illustrates the importance of divining the ancestral will. In this story, the Empress Jingū carries out her religious functions by transmitting the ancestral will to her husband, Chūai, the fourteenth emperor. Due to his disbelief and consequent death, however, the Empress is eventually forced to execute that will herself by launching an attack on Korea.

> This Empress, Her Augustness Princess Okinaga-tarashi [Empress Jingū], was at that time divinely possessed. So when the Heavenly Sovereign [Emperor Chūai], dwelling at the palace of Kashihi in Tsukushi [Kyūshū], was about to smite the land of Kumaso [roughly present Kumamoto Prefecture], the Heavenly Sovereign played on his august lute, and the Prime Minister the Noble *Take-uchi,* being in the pure court, requested the divine orders. Hereupon the Empress, divinely possessed, charged him with this instruction and counsel: "There is a land to the Westward [Korea], and in that land is abundance of various treasures dazzling to the eye, from gold and silver downwards. I will now bestow this land upon thee." Then the Heavenly Sovereign replied, saying: "If one ascend to a high place and look Westward, no country is to be seen. There is only the great sea;" and saying, "they are lying Deities," he pushed away his august lute, did not play on it,

and sat silent. Then the Deities were very angry, and said: "Altogether as for this empire, it is not a land over which thou oughtest to rule. Do thou go to the one road [that of death]!" Hereupon the Prime Minister the Noble *Take-uchi* said: "[I am filled with] awe, my Heavenly Sovereign! Continue playing thy great august lute." Then he slowly drew his august lute to him, and languidly played on it. So almost immediately the sound of the august lute became inaudible. On their forthwith lifting a light and looking, [the Heavenly Sovereign] was dead.

Kojiki (Translation by B.H. Chamberlain)

Stories such as this point to the importance of ancestral advice in the political decisions of ancient Japan. By virtue of being able to communicate with their ancestors, the emperors were believed to transmit divine commands; hence the title of *mikoto* (august words) given to early rulers, who were venerated as living gods.

The story of Empress Jingū, fiction albeit so far as many scholars are concerned, indicates the end of the duality of religious and secular rule in Japan. She later placed her son Ōjin on the throne who, because he had no brothers or sisters, combined both imperial functions. He duly married and his eldest son in turn continued the one-person rule introduced by his father. Since a period now begins in which the Yamato Court entered into relations with Korea and China, it is not unreasonable to presume that the Japanese emperors were emulating the Chinese emperors, who made no distinction between the religious and secular functions of their rule.

The emperors achieved the abolition of dual emperorship at the cost of increasing dependency on the clans however. Ōjin and his successors were forced to stay within the palace confines as had the priest-emperors before them in order to maintain the ritual purity necessary to fulfull their religious functions. Reluctant to conduct military campaigns or to deal with other political matters requiring attention outside the palace, the emperors had no choice but to delegate matters to prominent clan members. As the clan leaders conducted the business of the nation their influence swelled until the emperors were reduced to little more than figureheads. It was, however, mainly due to the religious functions that the imperial institution was able to survive until modern times.

EMPERORS AND LOCAL DEITIES

Shintō had considerable influence on the political organization of the Yamato state, for belief in local deities as opposed to one central Being precluded the idea of the allegiance of all people to a supreme ruler and tended instead to promote local autonomy or, at best, a compromising feudalism. Local chieftains often defied imperial authority. Judging by the fear and respect emperors had to manifest toward local divinities, it is clear that they had no absolute authority over their land, nor over the local clans that worshipped these deities.

Emperor Yūryaku and the deities of Mt. Katsuragi and Mt. Miwa: The Emperor Yūryaku (r.457-489), who is described in Chinese chronicles as a powerful sovereign ruling wide areas of both Japan and Korea, once had to hastily climb a tree in the mountains of Katsuragi to save himself from the onslaught of a local deity in the form of a boar. When Yūryaku ventured into the same mountains again, the same deity appeared to him in a different guise.

> Again once, when the Heavenly Sovereign [Yūryaku] made a progress up Mount Kadzuraki, the various officials were all clothed in green-stained garments with red cords that had been granted to them. At that time there were people ascending the mountain on the opposite mountain acclivity

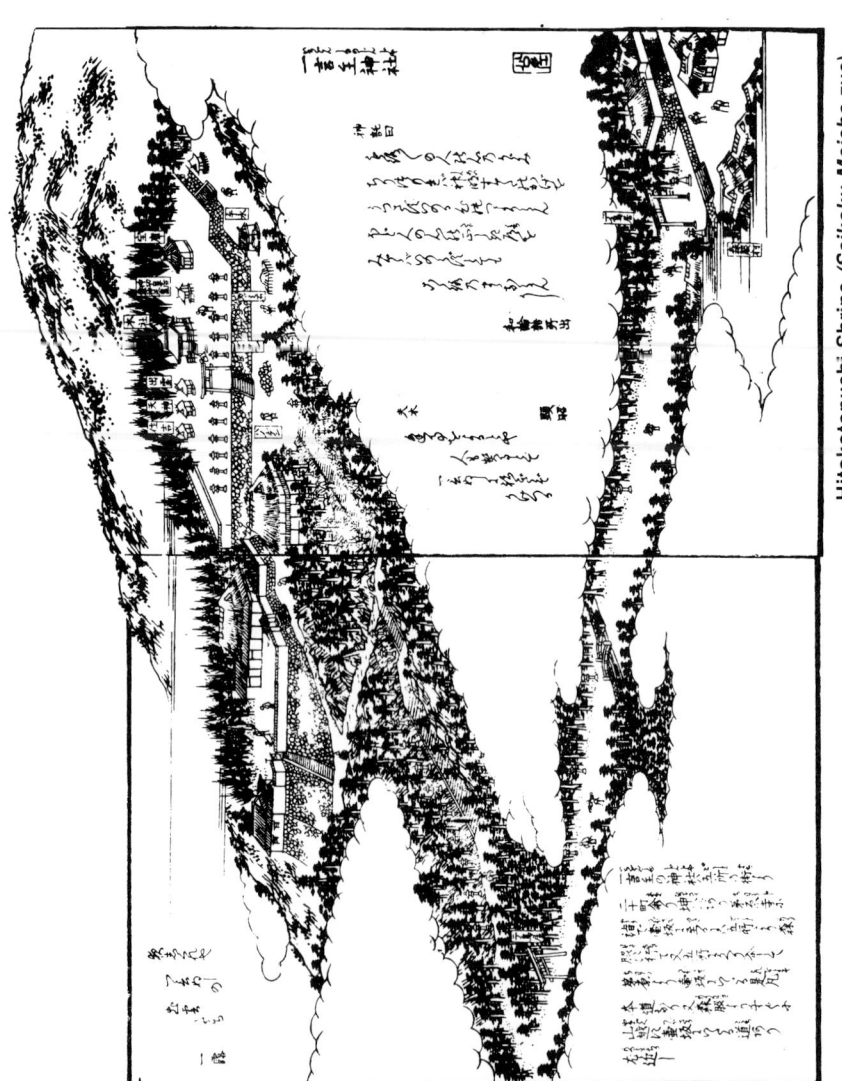

Hitokotonushi Shrine (*Saikoku Meisho-zue*)

quite similar to the order of the Heavenly Monarch's retinue. Again the style of the habiliments and likewise the people were similar and not distinguishable. Then the Heavenly Sovereign gazed, and sent to ask, saying: "There being no other king in Yamato excepting myself, what person goeth thus?" The style of the reply again was like unto the commands of a Heavenly Sovereign. Hereupon the Heavenly Sovereign, being very angry, fixed his arrow [in his bow], and the various officials all fixed their arrows [in their bows]. So the Heavenly Sovereign again sent to ask, saying: "Then tell thy name. Then let each of us tell his name, and [then] let fly his arrow." Thereupon [the other] replied, saying: "As I was the first to be asked, I will be the first to tell my name. I am the Deity who dispels with a word the evil and with a word the good, — the Great Deity of *Kadzuraki*, Lord of One Word." The Heavenly Sovereign hereupon trembled, and said: "I reverence [thee], my Great Deity. I understood not that thy great person would be revealed;" — and having thus spoken, he, beginning by his great august sword and likewise his bow and arrows, took off the garments which the hundred officials had on and worshipfully presented them [to the Great Deity]. Then the Great Deity, Lord of One Word, clapping his hands, accepted the offering. So when the Heavenly Sovereign made his progress back, the Great Deity came down the mountain, and respectfully escorted him to the entrance of the Hatsuse mountain. So it was at that time that the Great Deity Lord of One Word was revealed.

(Kojiki)

The "Great Deity Lord of One Word," Hitokotonushi in Japanese, is enshrined at the Hitokotonushi Shrine, situated in the Katsuragi mountains, which is still among the famous shrines of the Yamato Plain.

On another occasion, Yūryaku, wishing to control the deity of Mt. Miwa, ordered that it be brought to him for inspection:

> The Emperor commanded Sukaru Chihisako Be no Muraji, saying: — "It is our desire to see the form of the Deity of Mimuro Hill [Mt. Miwa]. Thou dost excel in strength of body. Go thyself, seize him, and bring him here." Sukaru answered and said: — "I will make the attempt, and go to seize him." So he ascended the Hill of Mimuro and caught a great serpent, which he showed the Emperor, who had not practised (religious) abstinence. Its thunder rolled, and its eyeballs flamed. The Emperor was afraid, and, covering his eyes, would not look upon it, but fled into the interior of the Palace. Then he caused it to be let loose on the Hill, and giving it a new name, called it Ikadzuchi (Thunderbolt).
>
> *(Nihon Shoki)*

It is apparent from stories such as these that emperors had to be respectful of local deities and, even after their territories were subdued, worship the divinities regularly so as not to provoke their wrath.

Political alliances and disturbances: In ancient Japan frequent conflict erupted between the emperors, who by nature sought to increase the territory under their control, and the local chieftains, who probably because of the religious independence of the local deities, ruled supreme over their own provinces. Although the emperors absorbed more and more land, they were forced to compromise with local religious power by customarily paying hommage to the deities of the defeated people and by appointing priests to chant prayers in which the conquered divinities were hailed as relatives of the emperor. While this appeased the divinities, the inability of the emperors to eliminate them altogether prevented enslavement of the conquered people. This practice was behind the reluctance of the Japanese, especially in early times, to exterminate entire clans. The imperial conquerors preferred instead to appoint the conquered chieftains as petty officials, integrating them into their hegemony.

The conflict between imperialism and local authority gave rise to a feudal state in the Yamato Plain. The early Japanese emperors, unable to impose themselves as autocrats or to centralize the state, depended on political alliances rather than on central authority for their ability to rule. The Katsuragi dynasty emperors were able to establish themselves in the Katsuragi area only by virtue of allying themselves with the Katsuragi clan through marriage with their daughters, a policy later emperors would employ. In view of the ritual necessity of abandoning polluted capitals, emperors also sought to transfer their palaces to land held by political allies, or by the empress's clan; imperial marriage was, therefore, a highly political concern.

One such alliance between emperor and local power dates back to Emperor Kaika, the ninth emperor, who was able to remove his capital from Mt. Katsuragi to central Yamato by marrying a woman of northern Yamato's Mononobe clan. Yūryaku, in order to rule without interference from his family, went so far as to kill all his brothers, appointing in their stead officials from powerful clans to carry out his orders. Alliances such as these were one of the means employed by emperors who ruled following the collapse of the dual sovereign system.

EMPERORS AND THEIR TOMBS

In spite of successional struggles and the necessary political alliances which prompted them, the emperors appear to have grown appreciably more powerful between the fifth and the seventh centuries and to have expanded their territory. The enlarged sizes of the imperial tombs attest to their growing ascendancy. Following the first, moderately small tumuli, larger ones appeared; and they grew to awesome sizes by the seventh century, pointing to the greater numbers of corvée laborers the emperors could call upon. Emperor Sujin's tomb, with two mounds that formed a keyhole shape, measures 100 meters from east to west and 200 meters from north to south. The tomb of the twelfth sovereign, Emperor Keikō, has a circumference of about one kilometer. The tomb of Emperor Ōjin is four hundred and twenty meters long with two mounds of 34 and 35 meters in height. The entire tomb is surrounded by a moat; apparently there were two moats originally. The largest tomb, said to have taken some 20 years to build, is that of Emperor Nintoku, Ōjin's successor. Also in the keyhole shape, it measures about 186 meters in length by 35 meters in height, attesting to the puissance of Nintoku with which he summoned local chieftains at will.

Early Japanese emperors were not cremated until Buddhism became firmly ensconced but were buried in tombs or mounds. Emperor Suinin, eleventh emperor of Japan, is credited in the histories with abolishing the practice of burying imperial servants alive with their deceased masters, and replacing them with clay figures called *haniwa*. Actually, although early texts mention the burial of living persons, there is as yet no archaeological evidence to support this. A large number of *haniwa* clay figures have been discovered in tombs. They are miniature replicas of, among other things, horses, houses and boats. These, together with the jewels, bronze mirrors and bells which have been unearthed in great numbers, provide us with an insight into the daily lives of the early Japanese emperors. Some of the tombs have even revealed wall paintings reminiscent of similar frescoes in Korean tombs.

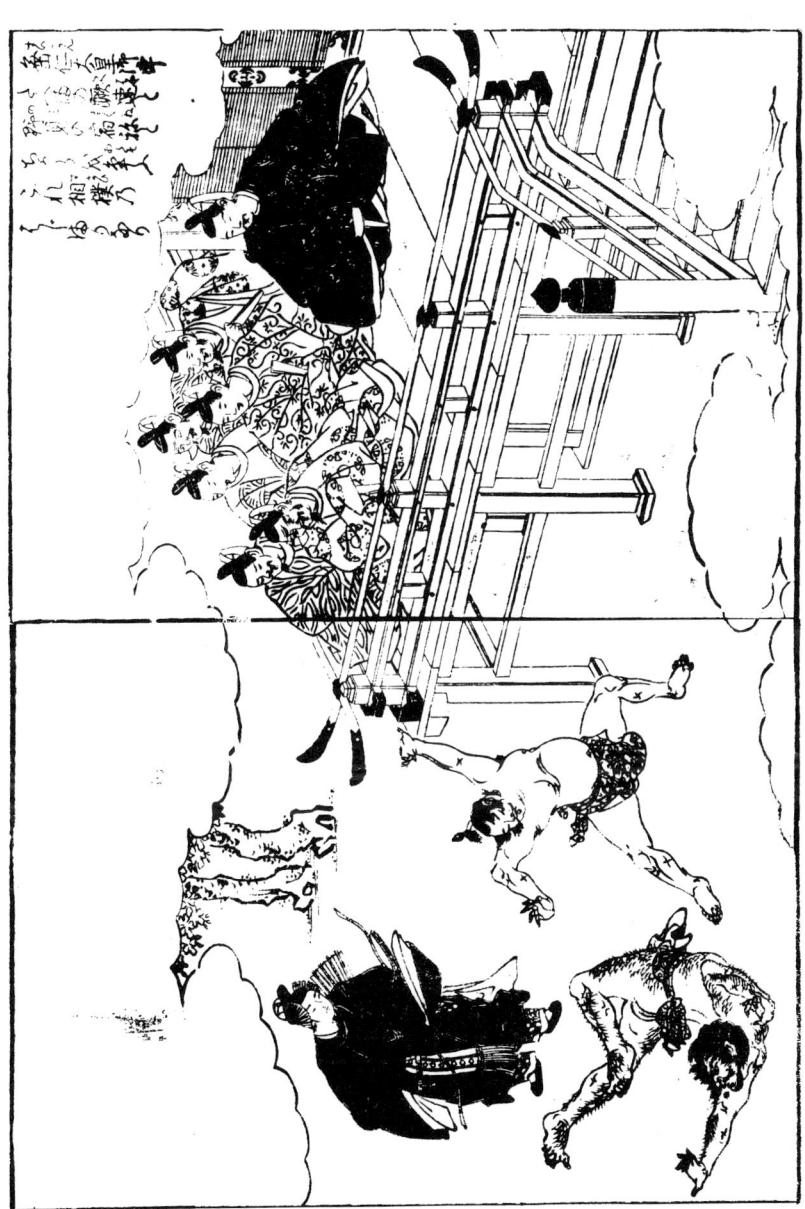

Sumo Wrestling under Emperor Suinin (*Yamato Meisho-zue*)

22

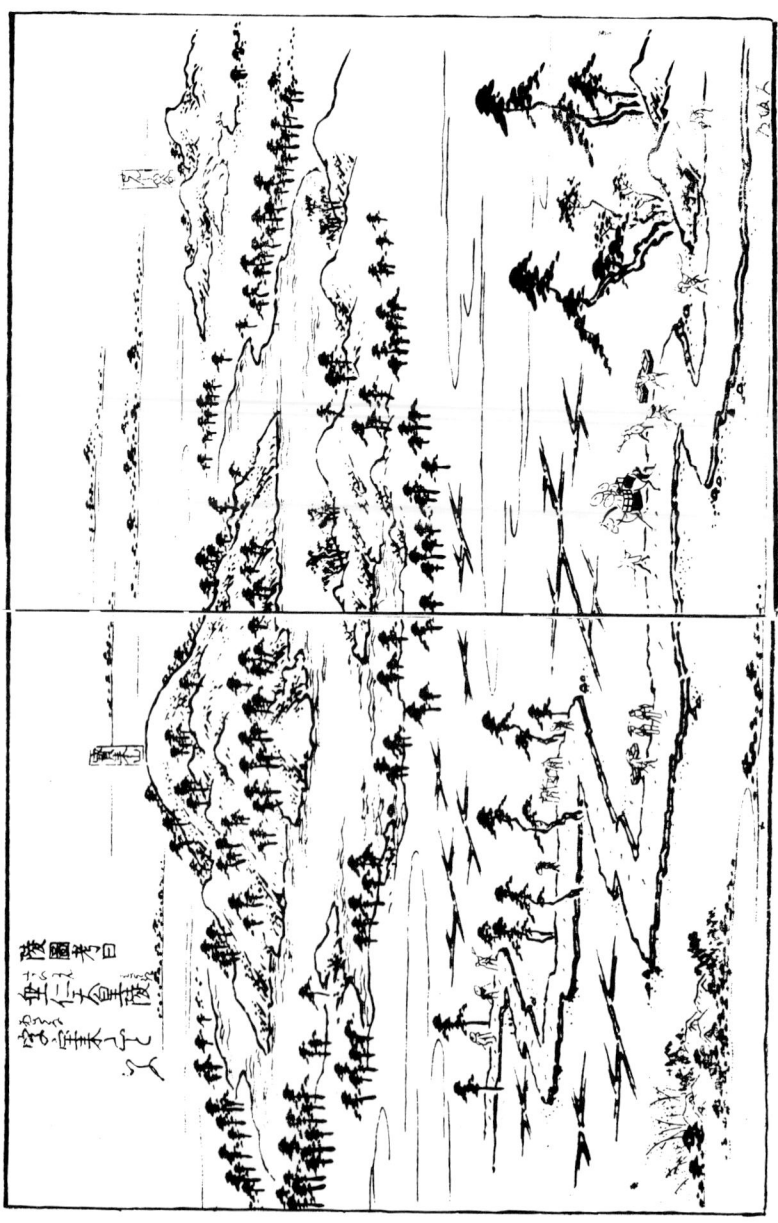

Emperor Suinin's Tomb (*Yamato Meisho-zue*)

OLD SHRINES OF YAMATO

The early history of ancient Shintō shrines, a blend as it is of myth and fact, is very vague. We know that they were accorded ranks of importance based on the power of the deity enshrined, but neither the specific reasons behind their erection or the approximate dates at which they were constructed have been recorded for posterity. Myths surrounding the shrines abound, however, and although their pasts are obscure, many of the shrines on the Yamato Plain are nonetheless important both religiously and historically.

Takamahiko Shrine: As previously discussed, emperors were compelled to worship the local deities of the territories on which they settled. With time, many of these divinities had come to be regarded as the ancestral deities of the clans in the area. So, for example, when Jimmu established himself at the foot of Mt. Katsuragi, he duly paid hommage to both the local divinities and to Takamahiko (also Takamimusubi), the deity from whom the Katsuragi clan claimed descent. Takamahiko was, according to the *Kojiki*, one of the deities who came into existence with the creation of heaven and earth, prior even to Izanagi and Izanami, the divinities credited with the creation of the Japanese islands. He was worshipped in an area called Takama (High Plain of Heaven) which lies partway up Mt. Kongō, one of the peaks of the Katsuragi mountain range. Takamahiko was not only an ancestral deity but also a local deity which may explain the local rather than the national nature attributed to these deities in strongly nationalistic pre-war Japan. It was not known for certain when the shrine was built to enshrine Takamahiko, but even before its existence, as long as the emperors resided in this area the entire mountain was revered as his sacred grounds. Because of the importance of Takamahiko, later emperors bestowed upon this shrine a very high rank.

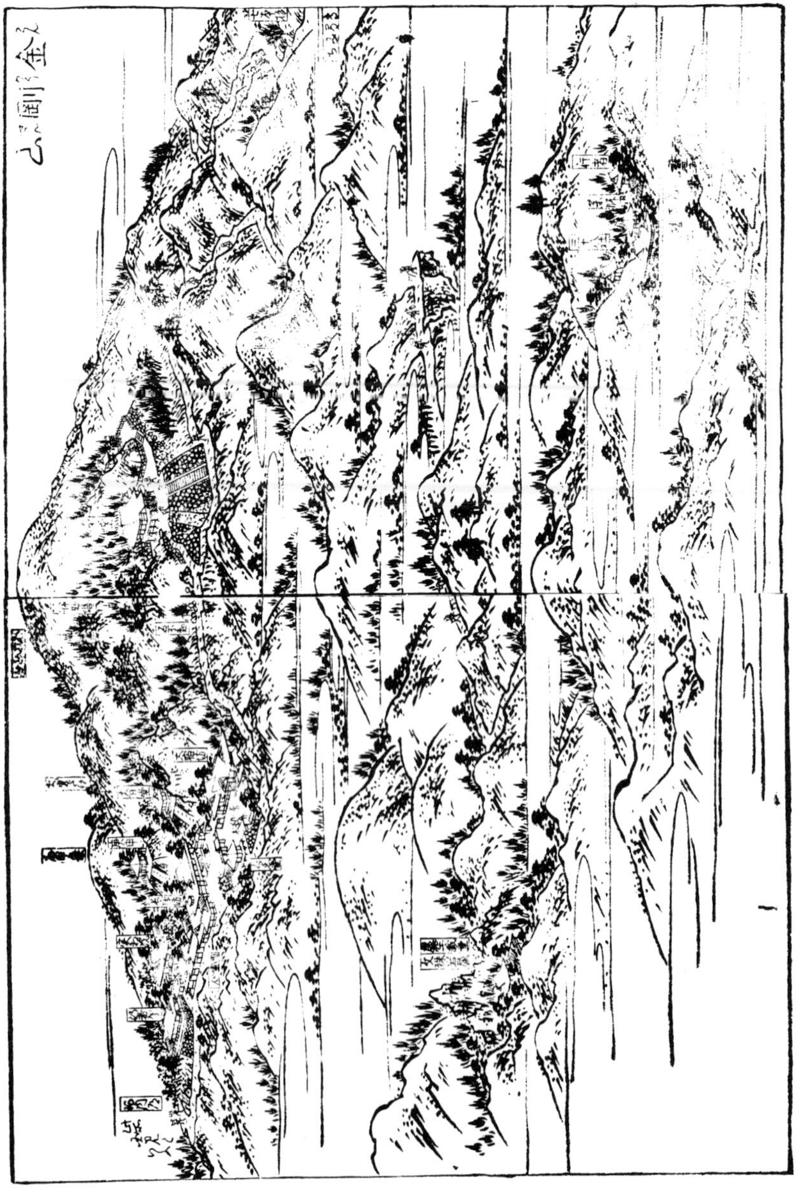

24

金剛山

Mt. Kongō *(Yamato Meisho-zue)*

Miwa (also Ōmiwa) Shrine: Miwa Shrine is particularly noteworthy not only because it enshrines principal Japanese deities, but also because of the magnificent sacred mountain that rises up 467 meters in front of which it stands. Mt. Miwa has often been venerated as the deity itself. Emperor Sujin, the tenth emperor, was the first to firmly establish himself in the area of Mt. Miwa and to build a palace there in the fourth century. It was then that the deity of Miwa, once just one of many local Yamato divinities, became the plain's most powerful deity and the protector of the imperial palaces built at the foot of the mountain. Frequent natural calamities had been besetting the Yamato Plain prompting Sujin to call all local deities to assemble. He made a divination to discover the causes of these calamities after which one of the deities promised to cease the calamities in return for receiving proper worship. When Emperor Sujin asked the divinity to reveal its name, it said: "I am the God who dwells within the borders of the land of Yamato, and my name is Oho-mono-nushi no Kami." *(Nihon Shoki)* The Emperor then decreed that it be enshrined at Mt. Miwa.

A deity's power, and by extension its territory, was thought to dwell in its name, according to the belief in "Word Souls." Revelation of its name, therefore, was equivalent to giving away that power or territory. (The story of the Great Deity Lord of One Word [Hitokotonushi] can be interpreted in this way also.) It also signified a deity's willingness to transform itself into a calm or peaceful deity, and the protector of the people who settled on its territory. Local deities often disclosed their names and ceded their territories on the condition that they receive proper hommage, but if this worship was neglected, they reverted to the rough, uncontrollable aspect of their natures wreaking havoc on all from the peasants to the emperors.

When sometime in the sixth century the territory of Izumo (present-day Shimane Prefecture) was appropriated by the Yamato court, the old Izumo deity was enshrined at Mt. Miwa as a placatory gesture. The emperor was then able to rule over Izumo by worshipping its deity. The transfer to Miwa of the Izumo deity is an

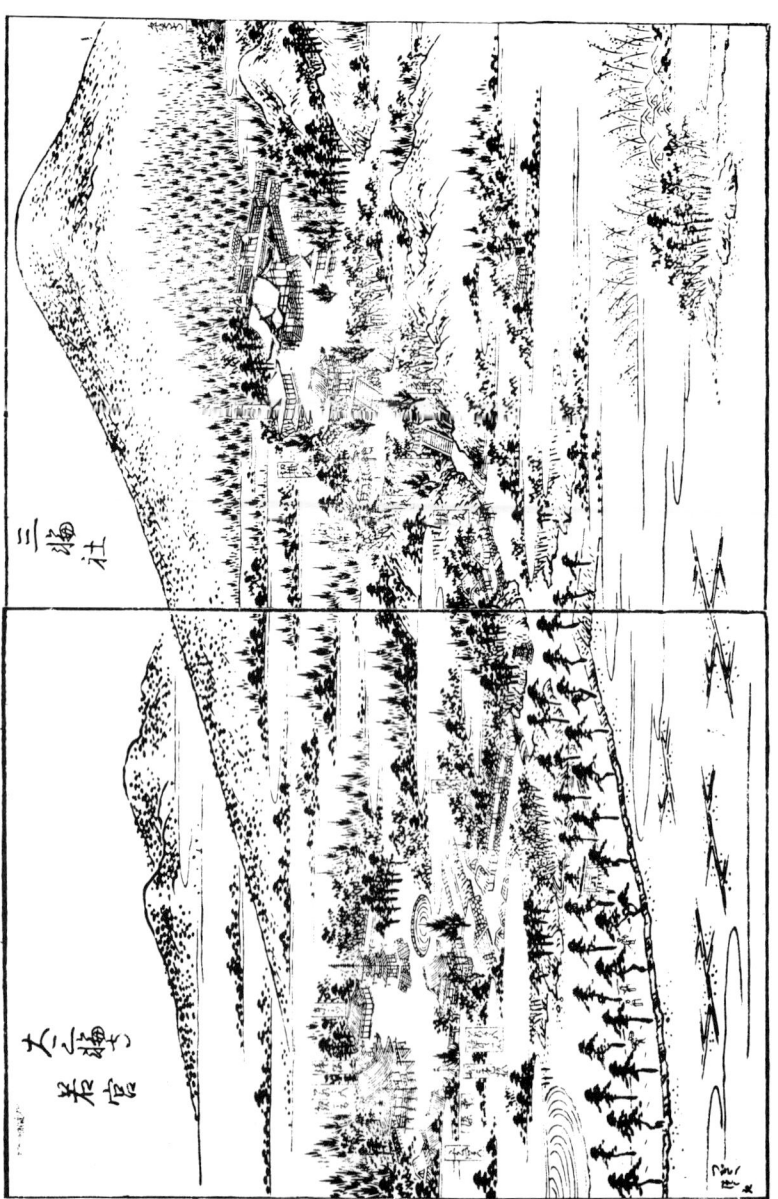

大神（おほみわ）神宮

三輪社

Miwa Shrine *(Yamato Meisho-zue)*

early example of attempts to concentrate all local divinities in a single location near the capital so the emperor could conveniently worship them.

While the Japanese rulers resided near Mt. Miwa the mountain came to symbolize home and was a point of orientation and protection for the traveller. The following poem exemplifies this:

On the Occasion of (Princess Nukada's) Journey to Omi

O that sweet mountain of Miwa —
I would go lingering over its sight,
Many times looking back from far upon it
Till it is hidden beyond the hills of Nara
And beyond many turnings of the road;
Then should the clouds be heartless
And conceal the mountain from me?

Envoy

Must they veil Mount Miwa so?
Even clouds might have compassion;
Should ye, O clouds, conceal it from me?

(Manyōshū)

The present Miwa Shrine sanctuary dates from the Edo Period but as an institution Miwa is Japan's oldest shrine.

Isonokami Shrine: "Country Pacifying Sword (Kunimuke no Tsurugi)," the symbol of the deity Futsumitama enshrined at Isonokami Shrine, is reputed by legend to have been sent by Takemikazuchi, the ancestral deity of the Mononobe clan, to aid Emperor Jimmu in subduing the tribes of the Yamato Plain. Jimmu enshrined the sword in his palace (apparently situated in what is now

28

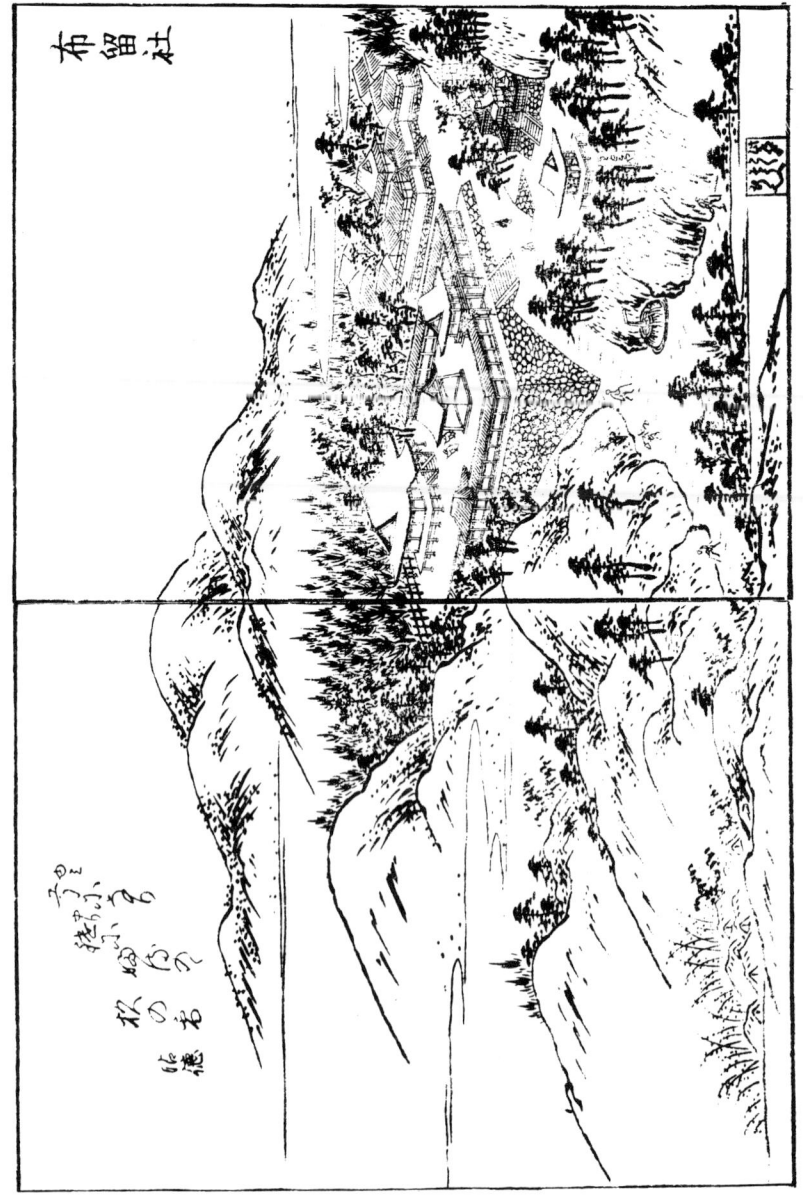

布留社

Isonokami Shrine (Furu-sha) *(Yamato Meisho-zue)*

Kashihara City), but it was transferred to Isonokami Shrine by Emperor Sujin and later placed in the care of the chief of the Mononobe clan in whose territory the shrine was built.

This is also the shrine where Sujin's successors and their military allies the Mononobe would ritually put to rest their "rough" war-waging souls during times of peace. Empress Jingū put to rest here the Shichishi, a sword serrated with seven spike projections which she is supposed to have procured during her military campaign against the Korean kingdom of Silla (Shiragi in Japanese). According to the *Nihon Shoki*, however, it was presented to the Empress by a Paekché envoy in 372 to mark the opening of the first official relations between Japan and the Korean kingdom. An inscription on the sword, that is dated 369, reads:

"By this there will be no more wars between us. It is good for the kings [portion illegible]. Until now, the Kings of Paekché had no sword like this. We made this according to the wishes of the Wa [Japanese] King. We hope that it will last for many generations."

This inscription, in Chinese, is one of the oldest traces of writing to have been found in Japan.

The main sanctuary, Haiden, at Isonokami Shrine is a reconstruction of the original dating back to the Kamakura Period (1185-1333) and is a National Treasure. The original sanctuary was an imperial palace building donated in 1081. Among the subsidiary shrines in its precincts is another National Treasure, the Izumo Takeo Shrine dedicated to the Izumo deity Izumo Takeo.

Yamato Shrine (Yamato Meisho-zue)

INTRODUCTION OF BUDDHISM

BUDDHIST TEACHINGS

This picture of the unstable early Japanese nation contrasts sharply with the image of a fiercely independent and at times isolated nation with which we are more familiar from recent Japanese history. In the Yamato (sometimes Tumuli) Period, c. 300-645, Japan was in closer contact with the Asiatic mainland, Korea in particular, than in most later historical periods. Historians have attempted to demonstrate that this contact had a considerable impact upon the development of Japanese civilization and the strength of the Yamato state.

China, Korea and Japan: Even before the Yamato Court was established, Japan and China were closely linked, and before a writing system was introduced into Japan enabling the Japanese to record their own annals, official Chinese histories described the nation. These histories provide the first record of Japan's existence. They also reveal the close official ties that existed between the ancient Japanese and Chinese. Once firmly established on the Yamato Plain, Japanese rulers sought diplomatic recognition by China, probably in order to legitimize their imperialistic design over local autonomy. The *History of the Sung Dynasty,* which covers approximately the fifth century, records several official Japanese missions to China, and reveals that Yamato emperors ruled over a large portion of southern Korea in addition to the Japanese islands.

Although early Japanese rulers maintained diplomatic relations with China from about the second century A.D. onward, they were more closely allied with Korea; when the three Korean kingdoms were founded after the Chinese lost control over Korea at the end of the third century A.D., the Yamato rulers established especially close ties with the Korean Kingdom of Paekché (Kudara in Japanese). Their armies often fought alongside one another, and Japan even settled a small colony called Mimana for Paekché's protection at the southern tip of the Korean peninsula in approximately 367. The Kingdom of Silla destroyed this colony in 562, unifying Korea and driving out the Japanese and their Paekché allies. Having lost its foothold in Korea, Japan's rulers were forced to concentrate more on expanding their domination over their own islands and effectively governing them.

A considerable number of Korean immigrants settled in Japan between the time the Three Kingdoms were established and the Japanese enclave in Korea was lost. According to a legend recorded in the *Izumo Fudoki* (a geographical survey of Izumo Province, compiled 713) Korean land was pulled by a rope across the Japan Sea to Izumo to allow for more living space. This legend probably is a reference to Korean immigration into Izumo territory. Koreans, many of whom claimed Chinese ancestry, brought with them the new cultural and technological achievements of the mainland. The Japanese generally welcomed the new settlers, whose skills benefited the Yamato state enormously, and integrated them into Japanese society by giving them large areas of the Yamato Plain and surrounding land in which to settle. By the ninth century, one-third of the central nobility had come to consist of originally immigrant families.

The innovations the Korean settlers brought included new techniques in agriculture, sericulture, irrigation, astronomy, medicine, architecture, and accounting; and in crafts such as brewing, brocade-weaving and silver and gold-smithing. They also introduced the Chinese writing system and Buddhism. Many a Korean family established its family temples on Japanese soil. Arm in arm with these came the political and ethical thought of China that would revolutionize Japan's social and political organization by the seventh century.

Korean immigration and Japanese contact with the mainland also opened Japan to the cultures of the Asian continent. Japanese embassies to China and Korea together with Korean immigrants allowed the Silk Road linking East Asia with India and the Middle East to connect with Japan, and thus a considerable amount of Mediterranean, Middle Eastern, Central Asian and Indian culture flowed into the country.

Hinayana (Lesser Vehicle) Buddhism: By the time Buddhism reached Japan in the sixth century, it had already been divided into two main teachings, both of which were to have a profound impact on the nation. Hinayana, or the Lesser Vehicle, was based on the life and teachings of the historical Buddha Shaka, who before attaining Buddhahood was an Indian prince (c. 563-483 B.C.) named Gautama who lived most of his life in the north of India. Becoming acutely aware of the sufferings and disease he saw around him and realizing the futility of social life as well as the shadow of death hovering over all living creatures, Gautama abandoned his home and family to dedicate himself to the search for the true meaning of life. While sitting in meditation, he attained a state of spiritual enlightenment and discovered that suffering, inherent in life, is caused by clinging to life and lustful cravings. He taught that if one is unable to free oneself from passion and indulgences such as sexual desire and craving for the pleasures of the moment, the consequence may be endless reincarnations as animals or beasts on earth or even in another world. Gautama taught that these cycles of life and death were in themselves the root of suffering.

In order to deliver one's self from suffering and undesirable reincarnations one must, Gautama taught, observe the so-called

Eightfold Path: Right View, Right Thought, Right Speech, Right Action, Right Livelihood, Right Effort, Right Mindfulness and Right Concentration. Strict observance of these precepts would lead to enlightenment, deliverance from the sorrows of existence and transmigration of the soul. He was, in effect, emphasizing spiritual purification by self-discipline. Adherence to these precepts would make it possible for one to become a saintly disciple of Gautama, the historical Buddha.

Mahayana (Greater Vehicle) Buddhism: The second stream of Buddhist teaching to reach Japan was called Mahayana, or the Greater Vehicle. Mahayana derived from the historical Buddha Gautama but regarded him as just one of many Buddhas who had appeared in many universes, all of whom were manifestations of one central Buddha and taught variously according to the needs in their different realms. The Lesser Vehicle taught that the Eightfold Path could be achieved only by those with the special ability to follow its eight tenets; whereas the Greater Vehicle made it clear that all sentient beings, animals, and plants could follow the Path and possessed, therefore, the potential for Buddhahood.

    Unlike Lesser Vehicle Buddhism in which the ideal was to become an *arhat* (in Japanese, Rakan), or saintly disciple of Buddha, the Greater Vehicle Buddhist strove to become a bodhisattva. A bodhisattva was one who, even having achieved the enlightenment and perfection necessary to become a Buddha, refused that state of bliss and, inspired by bountiful compassion, determined to serve and save other suffering mortals. The Greater Vehicle Buddhist relied for his salvation, then, on a variety of Buddhas and bodhisattvas whose wisdom and helpfulness were believed to be without bound.

    In order to categorize the various Buddhas and bodhisattvas, the Greater Vehicle developed the philosophy of the Three Forms of the Buddha. The first is his all-embracing, universal, cosmic form; the second is the transcendental form exemplified by Yakushi, the Healing

Buddha, Miroku, the Buddha of the Future, and Amida, the Buddha of Mercy; and the third is the Buddha Transformation Body, or the historical Buddha Gautama. The second form is the one in which he appears to the bodhisattvas and which artists represent in art and sculpture. The third form is his incarnation into a human being. All three Bodies belong to the one central and ultimate Buddha, Dainichi, who is manifested in all of them.

In trying to understand the ultimate reality of truth, Mahayana developed systems of highly abstract and speculative thought. Nagarjuna, a second century Buddhist philosopher, argued that the ultimate reality can only be expressed paradoxically as the Void or Emptiness — in other words, everything is essentially nothing. Two centuries later the philosophers Asanga and Vasubandhu contended that everything in the visible universe has no ultimate existence in itself but is a creation of our individual consciousness participating in a universal consciousness. Ultimate reality they called ''Suchness'' and ''Truly So,'' meaning that-which-is-as-it-is — another way of expressing reality while avoiding speculation in ordinary understandable language!

Another notable difference between the two streams of teaching was the geographical directions in which they travelled. The Lesser Vehicle spread towards Ceylon and Southeast Asia, while the Greater Vehicle turned toward Tibet, China, Korea and Japan and underwent, due to its liberal universalistic doctrine, considerable modification from country to country. Although the Greater and the Lesser Vehicles were introduced into Japan at the same time, the Greater Vehicle had a far stronger impact.

The adoption of Buddhism by Japanese clans: The introduction of Buddhism influenced Japan politically as well as spiritually. Initially Buddhism was the prerogative of immigrant families but with the growing involvement of Koreans in Japanese politics, some of the powerful native families embraced Buddhism and used the foreign

religion to justify their power. The Soga was one such clan. They rose
into prominence in the sixth and seventh centuries when they were
appointed as *omi* (chief ministers) by emperors who settled themselves
on Soga territory. In order to build up their strength, the Soga
encouraged Koreans to settle in Asuka, Soga territory, to the south of
the Yamato Plain. Hence it comes as no surprise that Buddhism took
its first foothold in this region under the sponsorship of the Soga.

The reasons why a powerful non-imperial clan would embrace a
foreign religion must be sought largely in sixth-century Japan's
political development. It was an age when religion and politics were
still closely intertwined and a legitimate state had to reflect the
spiritual persuasions of the nation. Buddhist cosmology, which saw
everything in the universe as a manifestation of a central cosmic
Buddha to whom everything was hierarchically subordinate,
supported a centralized state with an all-powerful ruler. This was in
sharp opposition to Shintō which tended to promote regional
autonomy and is quite probably one reason why Buddhism was
adopted by some clans.

THE FIRST TEMPLES

Shitennō-ji Temple and Buddhism versus Shintō: It can hardly have been
coincidental that the clans opposed to the Soga family were those
which served the emperors as Shintō ritualists and military allies.
Afraid of losing their hold over the imperial family, these conservative
clans favored the preservation of the old order, and in their ensuing
struggle against the Soga both their political and religious supremacy
was at stake.

We have seen that Buddhism entered Japan from the Asian
mainland; it was, in fact, Japanese interest in Korea that sparked the
rivalry between the two religions. Their struggle started in 556 when,

records the *Nihon Shoki*, in an effort to gain Japanese support for its fight against Silla, King Syŏng Myŏng of Paekché sent to the Japanese court a statue of the historical Shaka, cast in copper and plated with gold, and a number of volumes of sutras. The accompanying letter in praise of Buddhism read:

> "This doctrine is amongst all doctrines the most excellent. But it is hard to explain and comprehend. . . . This doctrine can create religious merit and retribution without measure and without bounds, and so lead on to a full appreciation of the highest wisdom. Imagine a man in possession of treasures to his heart's content, so that he might satisfy all his wishes in proportion as he used them. Thus it is with the treasure of this wonderful doctrine. Every prayer is fulfilled and naught is wanting. Moreover, from distant India, it has extended hither . . . where there are none who do not receive it with reverence as it is preached to them.
>
> Thy servant, therefore, Myŏng, King of Pèkché, has humbly despatched his retainer . . . to transmit it to the Imperial Country [Japan], and to diffuse it abroad throughout the home provinces, so as to fulfil the recorded saying of Buddha: 'My law shall spread to the East.' "
>
> *(Nihon Shoki)*

The Soga clan favored sending troops against Silla but met with stubborn resistance from the Shintō ritualists, the Nakatomi clan, and the conservative military clan, the Mononobe. Emperor Kimmei (r. 539?-571?) granted the campaign against Silla and also gave the Soga permission to worship the Paekché image privately. But when an epidemic that ravaged the country was attributed to the ritual pollution and evil influence of the foreign statue, Emperor Kimmei ordered the gold and copper Buddha thrown into the river in keeping with an old Japanese custom that all evil be floated downriver into the

The burning of a Buddhist temple by Mononobe no Moriya in A.D. 585 (*Saikoku Meisho-zue*)

ocean. The temple the Soga had built to shelter it was razed. Another statue brought to Japan by a Paekché visitor, was burned in 585 and the ashes cast into the river at the order of Kimmei's successor Bidatsu (r. 572?-585?) when Soga no Umako (d. 626), the leader of the clan, held a large-scale Buddhist ceremony conducted by monks and nuns descended from Korean families. As contention between the two faiths escalated, the emperors vacillated between the turmoil that might be unleashed with the destruction of the old Shintō-based order and the power they could gain with a centralized nation supported by Buddhist cosmology.

When both Emperor Bidatsu and the Mononobe chief fell ill shortly afterward, as though in punishment for their opposition, Umako advised the Emperor that the Three Buddhist Treasures alone — Buddha, Law and Priesthood — had the power to restore him to health. The Emperor rescinded his prohibition of the faith and permitted the Soga to worship again; he himself embraced Buddhism shortly before he died. His successor, Yōmei (r. 585-587), followed the native religion which for the first time became known as "Shintō" to distinguish it from the foreign "Buddhism." When, like his predecessor, he became sick, Yōmei ordered the making of a triad (a Buddha and his two attendants) as a prayer for his recovery. Unfortunately this triad no longer exists.

The Buddhist-Shintoist rivalry was finally decided in the year 587 in favor of Buddhism. In that year the Soga, supported by the military Ōtomo clan, eliminated the Mononobe and Nakatomi in battle. Since the fate of a religion in Japan was often dependent upon the fate of its advocate clans, the victory of the Soga and their allies meant the victory of Buddhism over Shintō. From that time forth, Buddhism met with little resistance from the Japanese court.

The story goes that during the battle, when the Soga were about to be routed, they ordered that statues of Shitennō, the Four Heavenly Kings who were the protectors of the Buddhist kingdom, be carved. The clan was trusting in the promise of the *Sutra of the Golden Light*

(Konkōmyō Saishōō-kyō)

> "If there are kings who propagate and study this precious
> *Sutra of the Golden Light*, we the Four Deva [Heavenly] Kings
> shall come to protect them always, and be with them at all
> times. Whatever calamities may befall or curses cast upon
> them, we the Four Deva Kings shall extinguish them.
> Eradicating all fears and pestilence from among them, we shall
> increase their longevity, and let them share in the propitious
> happiness of heaven. Their hearts' desires shall be fulfilled and
> there shall be an outpouring of joy. We shall also make all
> soldiers in their countries to become strong. . . ."
>   (Translated by John Lu in *Sources of Japanese History*)

The carving of the statues ordered, the Soga attacked with renewed
vigor and were able to defeat their enemies.

After their triumph the Soga built, according to the *Nihon Shoki*,
a temple to house the statues of the Heavenly Kings. Five years later,
another larger temple was built with the aid of temple carpenters,
roof-tile potters, a painter and a metal smith sent by Paekché to assist
in its construction. The end product was the Shitennō-ji Temple (now
in Osaka City), the architectural style of which had never before been
seen in Japan. Its impressive proportions, the harmony of the buildings
and its imposing beauty made an impression on the Japanese that
helped to solidify Buddhism's foothold in Japan.

The temple buildings were arranged according to Korean and
Chinese models along a north-south axis. The Chūmon (Middle
Gate), a pagoda, the Kondō (Main Hall) and the Kōdō (Lecture Hall)
all faced south towards the Daimon (Great Gate). The entire temple
grounds were encircled by a cloister, a covered walk with an open
colonnade that faced inwards to give the worshipper the impression of
having entered an entirely different realm; the realm of the Buddhas
safely remote from the ordinary world yet not inaccessible, as indicated

by the open south gate. The architectural harmony of the buildings and the visual symmetrical balance they created symbolized the new centrally controlled political order the advocates of Buddhism wished to institute using the new religion as its justification. The Lecture Hall was reserved for the study of Buddhist scriptures, a physical statement that temples were centers of learning and training rather than places for popular worship.

In contra-distinction to the flimsy Shintō shrine structures, intentionally so constructed to facilitate periodic rebuilding for ritual purposes, Buddhist temples were built to last longer. Even so, compared with the stalwart cathedrals of Europe, temples did not withstand the viscissitudes of history, or the fires, typhoons and earthquakes inflicted by nature. They have necessarily been restored and rebuilt on countless occasions over the centuries, although their original design has generally been preserved. The Shitennō-ji, damaged by a typhoon in 1934 and by the air raids of 1945, is still arranged today as it was 1400 years ago.

Asuka-dera (also Hōkō-ji) Temple and the victory of Buddhism: As an act of thanksgiving for his victory over the Shintō faction, Umako built another temple, this time in Asuka, in 588. Paekché was keen to nurture the budding of Buddhism in Japan and again provided temple carpenters, tile makers, painters and six priests to aid in its construction and, in addition, presented the Soga with relics of the historical Buddha Shaka. Asuka-dera Temple, modeled upon the layout and architecture of Paekché temples, was completed in 596 thanks to Paekché's assistance and the donation of gold by the King of the Korean Kingdom of Koguryŏ.

Pagodas, having derived from the Indian stupas built for the preservation of Buddha's relics, are symbols of the Buddha Shaka, and excavations have shown that the pagoda at Asuka-dera occupied the central position in the temple grounds indicating that worship there was centered on the historical Buddha. In harmony with the Buddhist

42

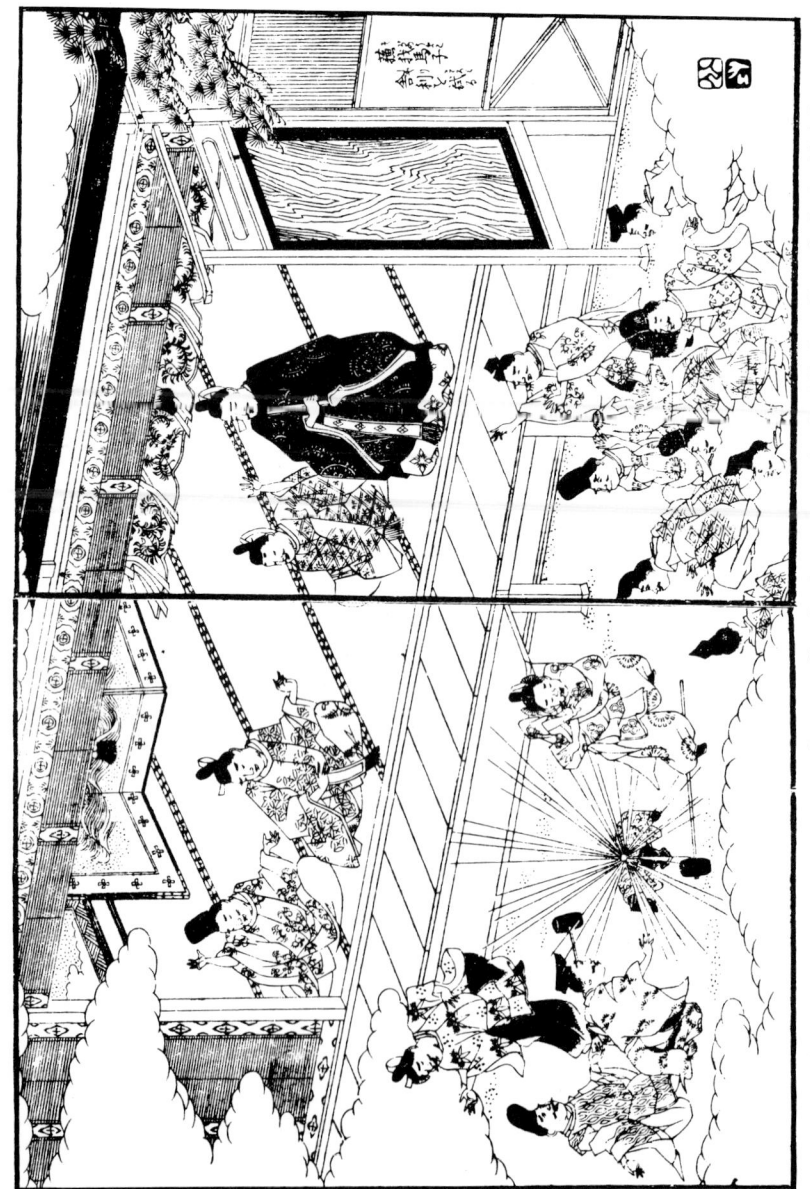

Soga no Umako inspecting the Buddha's relics (*Saikoku Meisho-zue*)

concept of the universe, a strict symmetrical balance was maintained in the organization of the temple's component buildings. Three Kondō (Main Halls) were positioned precisely around the pagoda, one to the east, one to the west and one to the north, and an avenue running from north to south divided the complex into two exact halves. A cloister connecting four gates and the Kōdō (Lecture Hall) centered in the north encircled the compound. Asuka-dera's main figure of worship was a large 2.75 meter high Shaka Buddha cast in bronze by a craftsman of Korean descent, Kuratsukuri no Tori (henceforth Tori). During the inauguration, an auspicious five-colored cloud is said to have engulfed the temple as a sign of its consecration by the Buddha.

The temple was later relocated in Nara where it is known today as Gangō-ji Temple. The bronze Shaka Buddha remains in its original Asuka location looking somewhat primitive in comparison with the more technically and artistically perfected statues of later periods that surround it. It has been repaired several times and the only original parts are the upper portion of its face, the left ear and three fingers of the right hand.

The erection of temples and the carving of statues was more than an act of faith on the part of the Soga clan. These were a physical defense of their newly acquired ability to assert control over the throne. The conservative Shintō faction ousted, the Soga were able to enthrone Empress Suiko* (r. 592-628) as their personal choice for ruler and in doing so gained greater leeway still in the handling of the political affairs of the nation.

Ishibutai (Dolmen) and Soga no Umako: As we have already seen, in abolishing the separation of rule between two rulers in favor of combining both ritual and secular functions under one sovereign, the emperors were forced to rely on the co-operation of powerful clans in national politics. The emperors became increasingly dominated by

---

* Suiko was the first empress recorded in Japanese histories.

these clans. Soga no Umako, for instance, maneuvered to control the throne by marrying his daughter to Emperor Jomei, a policy later families would also adopt in bids to command the imperial family.

Umako was instrumental in introducing Buddhism but was not cremated in accordance with Buddhist custom. He is thought to have been buried in a chamber of huge rocks called Ishibutai or Dolmen, which one can still see in the Asuka region. It is the largest grave of this type in Japan. The inner chamber measures 7.7 meters in length, 3.4 meters in width and 4.8 meters in height. It was originally covered by a huge earthen mound that no longer exists having in all likelihood been dug up and carried away by grave robbers.

SHŌTOKU TAISHI AND THE BIRTH
OF MODERN JAPAN

Shōtoku Taishi and Chinese civilization: The religious and political functions of the emperors were separated once again when the Soga appointed Empress Suiko's nephew as regent in 592. The regency fell upon Prince Umayado (posthumously Shōtoku Taishi, 574-622), one of the most important personalities in early Japanese history and a cultural hero in modern Japan. Little is known about Shōtoku personally except that he was Buddhism's staunchest advocate and under his guidance Buddhism flourished and was firmly implanted in Japan. Prince Shōtoku was an emperor's son and his mother and his concubine were Soga. With such close ties to the imperial family, the Soga sought to strengthen their position vis-a-vis other influential clans in order to firmly entrench Buddhism as a state religion and to modernize Japan along Chinese lines.

Developments in China undoubtedly influenced the reform of Japan in the seventh century for at that time China's civilization and political might had reached new heights under the Sui (589-618) and the early T'ang (618-907) dynasties. Japan modeled itself after China not because China threatened it to do so, but because the imperial family saw in the Chinese emperors, who ruled with the aid of a central bureaucracy, a possible means to strengthen its own position and thereby the nation's. The imperial and other leading families of Japan justified the reforms they wished to institute by pointing to the great Chinese achievements in political administration. The Chinese tended to consider their own accomplishments as the standard for all civilization and were reluctant to deal with nations that would not emulate these achievements. Consequently, Japan's leading clans also hoped that by introducing Chinese civilization they could bring China to recognize Japan diplomatically and thereby extend their authority over the nation.

So that Japan would not appear to the Chinese as a weak, politically unstable and culturally backward country, Shōtoku instituted a number of reforms before entering into official relations with China in 607. In 604, he formed an imperially appointed bureaucracy and adopted the Chinese calendar signifying a break with the old, complex cyclical time systems of Shintō in favor of a more historical, linear concept of time.* The new calendar meant that the Japanese would record their history as did the Chinese, who considered historical records vital to civilization. In the same year, Shōtoku promulgated the Seventeen-Article Constitution clarifying, on the basis of the Chinese concept that the sovereign is the ''Son of Heaven'' with absolute power, the relationship between emperor and subject as identical to that of heaven and earth. This constitution, Japan's first legal document, guided not only administration and justice but also the moral principles necessary to any benevolent government. It marked a movement away from the previous system of laws determined more or less by custom.

Shōtoku Taishi and Buddhism: The Seventeen Article Constitution officially confirmed Buddhism as a state religion. Shōtoku was a devout Buddhist personally, but he realized the powerful political tool

---

* The ancient Japanese believed that time travelled in circles. At intervals of a certain number of years, time would end and would have to be renewed by ritual means. These rituals (Shintō festivals) ensured a new start of time. Whereas in Buddhist thought it was impossible to return to time already lived through, according to Shintō custom, time eternally returned.

Buddhism had proved to be in China, supporting as it did the idea of an absolute monarch and unifying the nation as the common faith of culturally distinct groups and clans. Shōtoku sought spiritually and politically, then, to unify the nation on the basis of the Greater Vehicle school of thought. Relying for his authority on the concept of the Eternal Dainichi Buddha speaking through countless lesser ones, he declared: "A country does not have two lords, the people do not have two masters."

Shōtoku should not be condemned for using Buddhism as a political ideology, because the peace and well-being of a state was perceived in those early centuries as dependent on an existing harmony between heaven and earth. By stressing that everyone had an equal potential for Buddhahood, Shōtoku was able to de-emphasize the traditional clan system that promoted a social hierarchy so often at the root of political instability. He applied Buddhism to the state; he also tried indefatigably to understand Buddhism and its scriptures. Under the guidance of the Korean Priest Eji, who arrived in Japan in 595, Shōtoku made an effort, the first by a Japanese, to study these scriptures. He was well-versed in Chinese and wrote commentaries on the *Lotus Sutra,* the chief doctrine of which was the Eternal Buddha's all-embracing scheme of salvation; on the *Shōman-gyō* Sutra, which emphasized the One Vehicle and the bodhisattva ideal, and on the *Yuima-kyō* Sutra, a discussion on the model Buddhist citizen. These commentaries reached even into China, where they were used in a Chinese temple with notes added by a Chinese monk.

In order for Buddhism to be established as the Japanese state religion, temples needed to be erected and statues carved. Throughout Japanese history, new ideas have had to take form in building and rebuilding projects. This practice of construction may well have begun when Shōtoku realized that Japan's new political order needed to be tangibly demonstrated. Temples for family worship were already common, but it was under his sponsorship that the construction of official temples began. Japan entered a period of frenetic building. In

623, it was reported that there were forty-six Buddhist edifices, and during the Nara Period (710-784) alone, 361 more temples were erected.

Over and above its official nature, temple construction often fulfilled private purposes. Most early temples were built as personal prayers: for victory in war or political struggles, for the recovery of afflicted emperors or empresses, for the afterlife of the deceased, or for the placation of potentially malevolent spirits. Private and public aims were often combined in early Japan by powerful clans striving to extend their hegemony over the whole nation using Buddhism as their tool.

HŌRYŪ-JI TEMPLE

The original Hōryū-ji Temple: By the year 601, Shōtoku must have felt there was little likelihood that he himself would become emperor in-spite of the fact that he had once been the Crown Prince. Perhaps, too, a desire to avoid the intrigues of the increasingly Soga dominated court prompted his decision to build a retreat in the area of Ikaruga, the birthplace of his favorite consort. At Ikaruga, Shōtoku dedicated himself to the study of Buddhism and attracted a number of followers. In 607, in order to accommodate them, he built within the palace grounds a temple which came to be known as Ikaruga-dera. The same year, he enlarged the temple and commissioned the sculptor Tori to make a statue of Yakushi, the Buddha who vowed to heal all the sick who called upon him for help. In so doing, Shōtoku fulfilled a promise he made to his sick father, Emperor Yōmei, in 587 to build a temple dedicated to the Buddha Yakushi as a prayer for his recovery. In all probability the temple would not have been completed were it not for a donation from Empress Suiko in appreciation of a lecture Shōtoku had given her on the *Shōman-gyō* Sutra.

YAKUSHI, Hōryū-ji Temple

The many skilled craftsmen (many of whom were Koreans) Shōtoku had gathered together for this project, constructed the temple in the same fashion as the Shitennō-ji, according to the laws of strict symmetry applied to Chinese and Korean temples. The statue of Yakushi carved by Tori was installed in the Main Hall and became the central object of worship at Ikaruga-dera. The temple complex was inaugurated in 616 by Priest Eji in an elaborate ceremony, which

SHAKA TRIAD, Hōryū-ji Temple

included Gigaku, ritual dances of Chinese origin performed in Buddhist temples in which the participants wore masks, and the new name of Hōryū-ji (Buddhist Law Prosperity) Temple was bestowed upon it.

Priest Eji returned to Korea following the completion of the temple taking with him Shōtoku's commentaries on the three sutras. After his departure, Prince Shōtoku was beset by misfortune. In 621 his mother died, and a year later his favorite consort. Shōtoku followed her about a month later.

As a votive prayer for the repose of his father, Shōtoku's eldest son, Prince Yamashiro no Ōe, commissioned Tori to cast a statue of the historical Buddha Shaka. When the statue was completed, people came to believe that Shōtoku had in fact been a reincarnation of Buddha because they claimed his features could be distinguished in the statue's face. The statue, completed in 623 according to an inscription on the halo, represents Shaka in a sitting position attended by two bodhisattvas. Its triangular shape and the formal folds of Buddha's garment give the impression of gravity and stability. The large hands and compassionate face express the welcome Buddha gives all people, consoling them in their wordly sufferings. His halo is so broad it encircles even his attendants signifying that his radiance embraces everybody. This Shaka triad can also be found in the Main Hall, situated to the east of the Yakushi statue.

The new Hōryū-ji Temple: The Hōryū-ji burned to the ground after being struck by lightning in 670. Its priests found temporary lodgings in the nearby Hōrin-ji and Hokki-ji Temples, both of which had been founded by Shōtoku's son, Prince Yamashiro. Donations of land by people who held Shōtoku in high esteem made reconstruction of the temple possible about forty years later. The new Hōryu-ji was built slightly west of where the old temple had stood. Its layout deviated considerably from that of the original temple. The Main Hall and the pagoda were arranged not along a north-south axis but placed side by side on an east-west orientation so that both structures came into view immediately upon entering the grounds through the Chūmon (Middle Gate). The Middle Gate, with only two entrances, was very unusual; a third entrance reserved for members of the aristocracy, was conspicuously absent, reflecting Shōtoku's philosophy of the equality of all men. Two Kongō Rikishi (also Niō), guardians of the Buddhist universe, protected this gate. The one with the open mouth pronounced the first sound of the Sanscrit alphabet and the one with

NIŌ, Hōryū-ji Temple

the closed mouth the last sound, indicating the beginning and end of
all things. From the Middle Gate one looked directly ahead to the
Daikōdō (Great Lecture Hall) which lay at the far northern end and
was linked to the rest of the complex by the cloister. The entire
complex was turned ninety degrees so that the full length of the
temple's rectangular shape faced southward, the direction from which
the visitor approached.

A number of buildings not included in the old Hōryū-ji Temple
complex were erected. A Belfry was built in the northeast of the
compound, a Kyōzō (Sutra Repository) in the northwest, as well as

NIŌ, Hōryū-ji Temple

priestly quarters, a Treasury and a Refectory. The Sutra Repository became necessary as aristocrats began to donate sutras which they had themselves copied. The copying of sutras was considered an act of merit which, if accumulated, increased the likelihood of salvation.

The Main Hall was partially rebuilt with material saved from the former hall, and the Shaka Triad and the Yakushi found a new home under its beautifully gabled roof. The inner walls were painted with pictorial representations of the pantheon of Amida, the Buddha of Mercy; Yakushi; Shaka; Miroku, the Buddha of the Future; and other lesser deities. Unfortunately, these were severely damaged by fire in

54

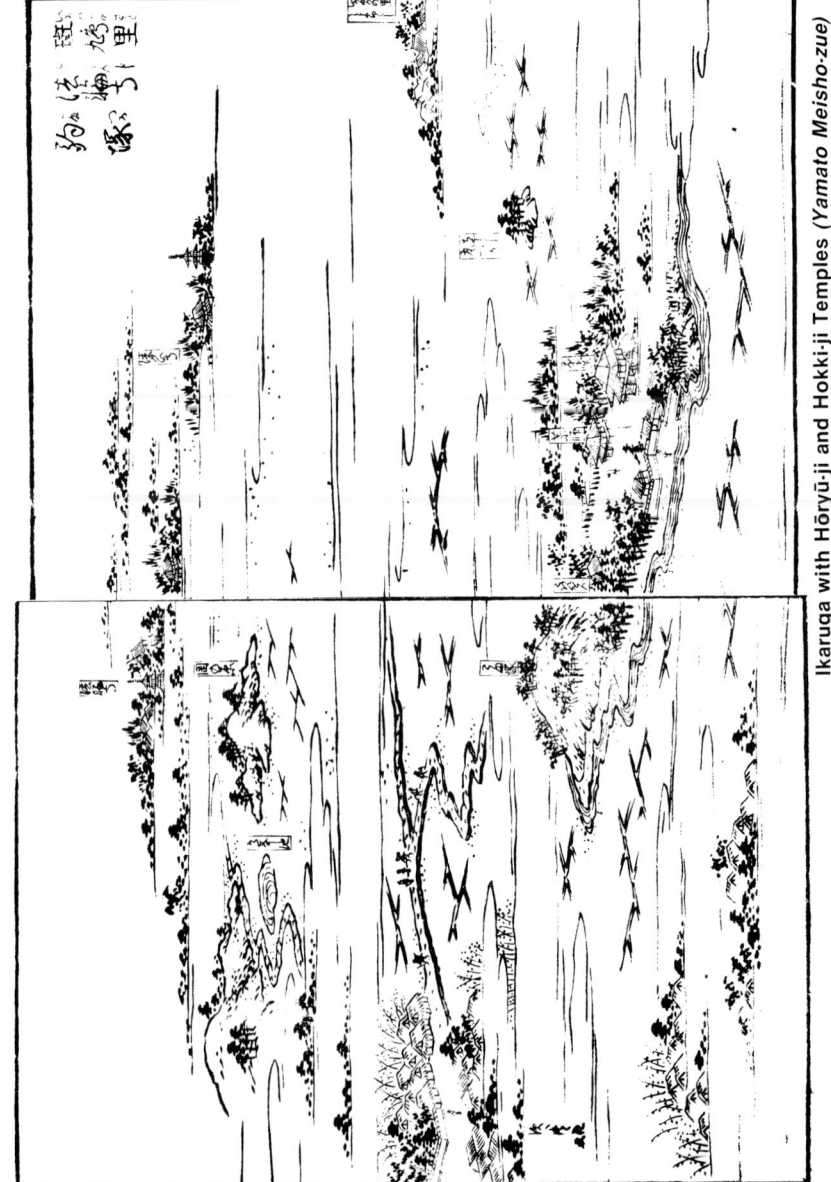

Ikaruga with Hōryū-ji and Hokki-ji Temples *(Yamato Meisho-zue)*

1949 though attempts to restore these are being made. Like the Main Hall, the rebuilt five-storied pagoda is one of the oldest extant wooden structures in the world. On the first floor one can see a chorus of Buddha's disciples lamenting the death of their master. These clay figures are arranged in a configuration similar to the contours of Mt. Sumeru, the central mountain in the Buddhist universe. These figures consist of four groups: to the north are Buddha's disciples lamenting his death and bodhisattvas attending the Buddha's entry into Nirvana; to the east is Yuima (Vimalakirti), one of Buddha's favorite disciples, conversing with Miroku; and to the west are disciples dividing Buddha's relics among themselves.

Tō-in (East) Temple and Sai-in (West) Temple: The Tō-in was a product of tragic and consequential political events that took place during the 25-odd years that elapsed after the completion of the new Hōryū-ji in 714. Emishi (d.645), Umako's successor as head of the Soga clan, rejected a bid by Shōtoku's son Yamashiro to become emperor and instead enthroned Empress Kōgyoku (r.641-645), wife of Emperor Jomei (r.628-641) in 641. Yamashiro retired to Ikaruga. The leaving of the capital by imperial princes was often interpreted as intention to gather forces to incite a rebellion. Such rebellions in the early history of Japan often led to bloodshed. Emishi and his son Iruka (d.645) treated Yamashiro's departure no differently and promptly dispatched troops to storm Ikaruga Palace. Yamashiro escaped first to Mt. Ikoma but, perhaps to avoid the bloodshed of innocent people, returned to Hōryū-ji Temple and there, in the very pagoda which one can still visit today, committed suicide together with all of Shōtoku's blood relatives.

Fearing that Shōtoku's soul might seek revenge for the elimination of his entire family, it was decided that the rebuilt Hōryū-ji was not sufficient appeasement but that in addition his Ikaruga residence should also be rebuilt as a temple. Among the concerned were the Empress Kōmyō (701-760), her mother, Lady Tachibana

56

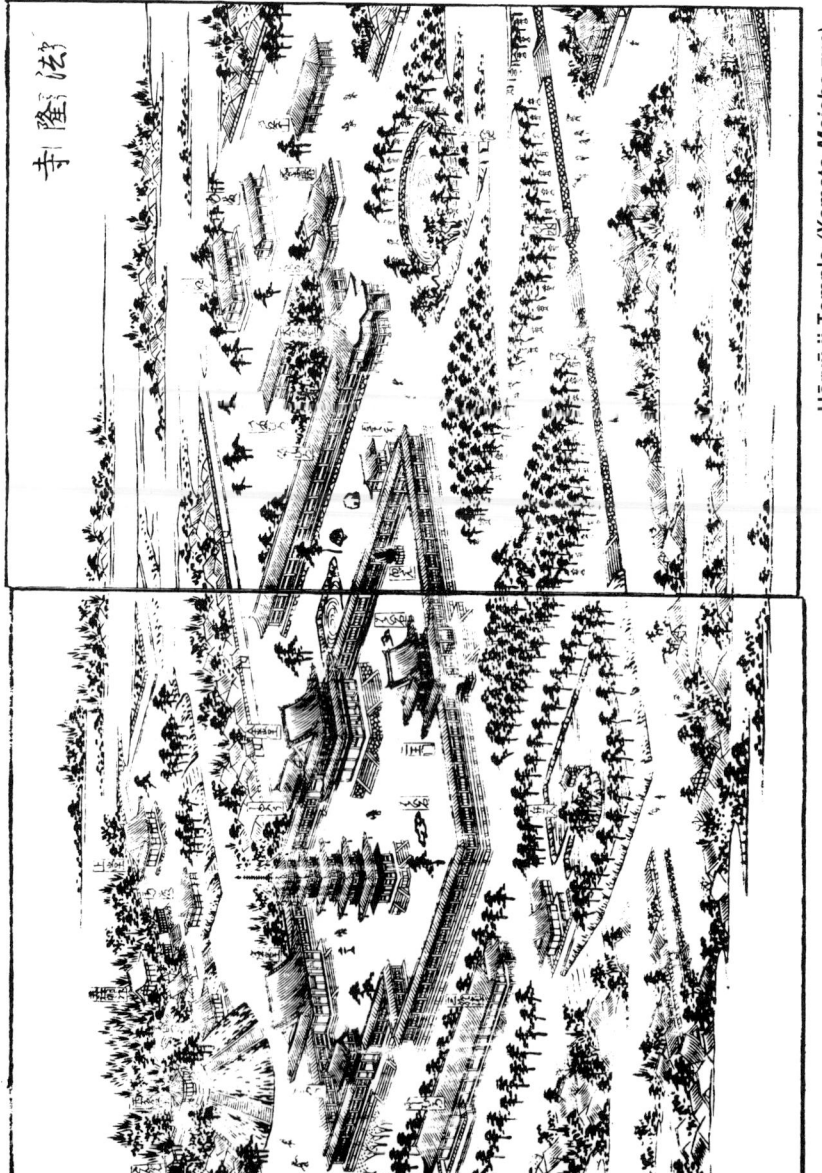

法隆寺

Hōryū-ji Temple (*Yamato Meisho-zue*)

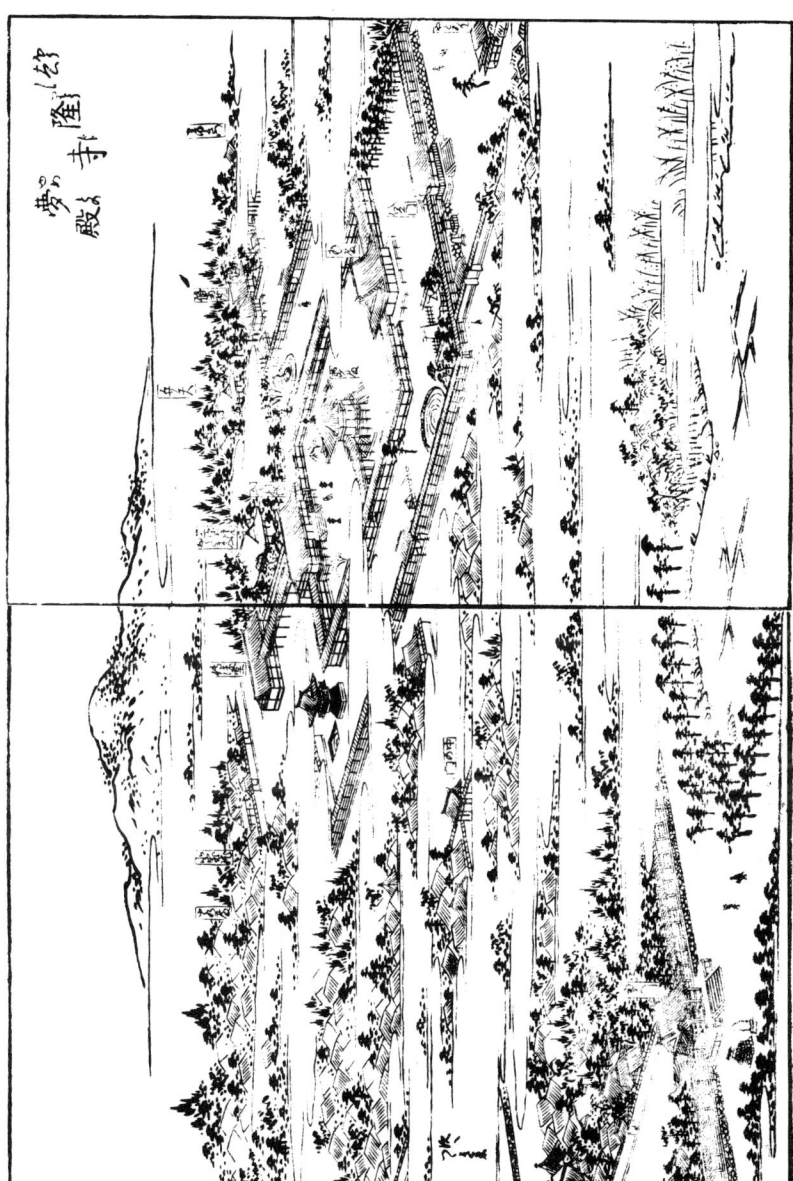

夢殿隆寺

Hōryū-ji Temple, Yumedono (*Yamato Meisho-zue*)

(d.733), who donated a building to the cause, and Priest Gyōshin (?-750), who supervised the transformation of the residence into a temple. The Tō-in was the end result in 739. It centered around an octagonal hall called Yumedono, or Hall of Dreams, that was dedicated to the memory of Prince Shōtoku. As its main figure of worship, a wooden Kuze Kannon was carved and placed on the very site where, legend has it, Shōtoku received divine inspiration when writing his commentaries on the three sutras. One tradition claims that when Shōtoku was unable to unravel the meanings of certain unintelligible passages an old man appeared to him in the dark of night revealing their mysteries. The Kannon, in a dreamlike state of meditation, holds in its hand a flaming gem, the symbol of the bodhisattva's power of salvation.

From this point on Shōtoku became the object of widespread worship throughout Japan. Convinced that he had become a bodhisattva and that his soul was living in a state of bliss within the Kuze Kannon, people worshipped the statue as the living Shōtoku. A recent theory sees in this statue and the manner in which the halo is nailed to its neck an attempt to prevent Shōtoku's soul from escaping to seek retribution for the tragic end met by his family by imprisoning it inside the statue.

A large space was left vacant in front of the Yumedono where memorial services could be conducted. Called Shōun-e, these services were usually carried out with great pomp. One recorded Shōun-e celebrated the four hundredth anniversary of Shōtoku's death in 1022. Because of the still flourishing Shōtoku cult, additional buildings were added on to the Tō-in complex on this anniversary and on the 500th anniversary.

The Kuze Kannon can still be worshipped today in the Yumedono. To the east of the Yumedono and contained in one building are the Edono (Picture Hall), which contains wall paintings portraying scenes of Shōtoku's life, and the Shari-den, the hall dedicated to the relics of Buddha. In the northern end of the complex

KUDARA KANNON, Hōryū-ji Temple

lies the Dempōdō (Transmission of the Law) Hall, the building that was donated by Lady Tachibana, and at the southern end, directly in front of the Nanmon (South Gate), is the Reidō (Prayer Hall).

Daihōzō-den (Treasury Hall):   The Treasury Hall, an independent unit of Hōryū-ji Temple, is a concrete building erected in 1939 to house the treasures accumulated by the Hōryū-ji during its long history. Of particular interest is the wooden Kudara (Paekché) Kannon, named after one of the Three Kingdoms of Korea because of its outlandish

YUMECHIGAI (DREAM-CHANGING) KANNON, Hōryū-ji Temple

features. It reflects southern Chinese style although it is actually of obscure origin. This bodhisattva of Mercy is possibly the work of the sculptor Tori. Its elongated proportions give the impression of the bodhisattva aspiring to paradisiacal heights while remaining on earth. Also in the hall is the Nara Period statue of Yumechigai Kannon, or Dream Changing Kannon, so called because prayers addressed to the deity were believed to change bad dreams into good ones.

The Tamamushi Shrine, the personal altar of Empress Suiko, is inlaid with murals made by the application of thousands of irridescent wings of the Tamamushi (Jewel Insect) beetle. On one panel the Buddha Shaka is portrayed in a previous life as a Brahman in India when he offered his life to a demon. On another panel, two angels hover over Buddha's disciples as they worship him. Mt. Sumeru is depicted on a third side. On the upper section of the altar, various other deities and bodhisattvas are depicted and the Buddha is shown preaching. Also on display here is the personal altar of Lady Tachibana on which the Buddha and his attendants are sitting on long-stemmed lotus flowers.

A number of statues in the Treasure Hall represent Prince Shōtoku at various ages. One shows him as a two-year old prodigy reciting "Hail the Buddha!" and another as a seven-year old beginning to study the sutras. A number of scrolls, painted portraits and a pictorial biography of Shōtoku are also on display, and there is even a wooden replica of his horse. All these works attest to the fact that it was primarily due to the popular worship of Shōtoku that Hōryū-ji Temple has survived until this day as a vestige of Japan's endeavor to modernize using Buddhism as its foundation.

Chūgū-ji Temple: The nunnery, Chūgū-ji, to the immediate east of the Tō-in was the residence of Shōtoku's mother. After her death it was converted into a temple dedicated to the repose of her soul. A wooden statue of Miroku, blackened by the incense burnt in offering before it for more than a thousand years, is preserved in the Main Hall. Included among Japan's most valuable art treasures, the statue represents the Buddha of the Future in deep meditation, his right leg crossed over and resting upon his left, and his right hand pointing pensively toward his chin. His face overflows with boundless compassion. According to Buddhist teaching, Miroku will remain a bodhisattva until he reappears at the end of the world to save mankind, fulfilling his destiny as Buddha of the Future. He will be the only Buddha other than the historical Buddha Shaka to appear on earth.

MIROKU BOSATSU, Chūgū-ji Temple (Photo by courtesy of Kintetsu)

Also preserved at the Chūgū-ji nunnery are fragments of the Tenjukoku Mandala* embroidered by one of Prince Shōtoku's concubines shortly after his death. It depicts imagined scenes of Shōtoku's soul in paradise. The Main Hall was renovated in 1968.

---

* Mandalas are pictorial representations of the Buddhist universe.

NAKATOMI (FUJIWARA) NO KAMATARI AND THE TAIKA REFORM

Shōtoku's reforms appear to have been aimed at strengthening the imperial family rather than the Soga clan. After his death, the Soga leaders chose to interpret his reforms to their own advantage. After eliminating Shōtoku's son Prince Yamashiro, who they perceived as a threat to their political ambitions, the Soga increasingly took upon themselves the prerogatives of the throne. They made and deposed rulers at will, they bestowed titles (an exclusively imperial right), they built huge tombs for themselves and had their palaces guarded by aborigines feared for their brutality.

Realizing the imminent threat to its existence, the imperial family secretly allied itself with the remaining Shintō ritualists, the Nakatomi clan, their military allies, the Mononobe, and with dissident factions of the Soga clan. In 645 a coup d'etat was successfully executed by the imperial prince Naka no Ōe, later to reign as Emperor Tenchi (r. 661-671), together with Nakatomi no Kamatari (614-669), the head of the Nakatomi clan. The empress, a Soga nominee, was deposed and succeeded by her younger brother with Naka no Ōe as heir apparent. As a reward for his services to the imperial cause, and perhaps also to free him from the Nakatomi's hereditary Shintō functions, the Emperor bestowed upon Kamatari the family name of Fujiwara, establishing him as the ancestor of a noble line that has continued to serve (and sometimes dominate) the emperors until the present.

Ironically, although the coup had been carried out by a traditional Shintō clan (the Nakatomi had continued their ritual functions) that had violently opposed the introduction of Buddhism, it did more to promote the foreign religion than to eliminate it. Both Kamatari and the prince must have realized that more than ever Buddhism was necessary for a stable state. There is no doubt, however, that the coup made it possible for Shintō practices to survive not only in the rural

Nakatomi no Kamatari and Prince Nakano Oe slaying Soga no Iruka *(Saikoku Meisho-zue)*

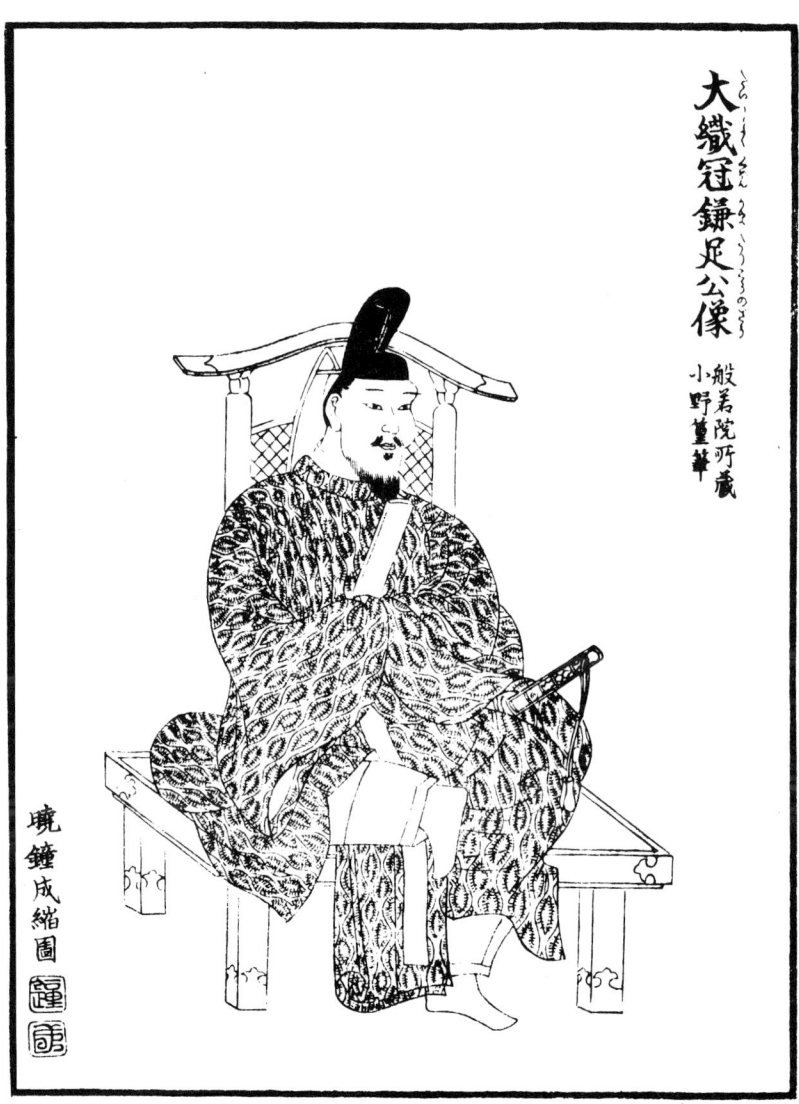

Nakatomi (Fujiwara) no Kamatari *(Saikoku Meisho-zue)*

areas but in the imperial court as well. Rituals such as the "Looking Down Over the Land" and the ancestral divinations had declined under the impact of Buddhism, although the Great Feast of Kingship rite had endured and emperors had continued to worship local deities.

The new leaders proceeded to sweepingly effect Shōtoku's visions of reform. They continued the missions to China Shōtoku had initiated, and relied heavily on the opinions and experiences of the students who accompanied the Japanese ambassadors to China where they studied, sometimes for several years. Using these students as a medium, Japan continued to import Chinese ways of thought, technology, art and government.

With the New Year celebrations of 646 began a fifty-year period of reforms that were to alter Japan radically. In that year, Emperor Tenchi instituted a universal system of taxation, he abolished all private ownership of land, redistributed it and established a permanent capital as the pivotal point of a system of provinces, districts and villages. These reforms, which gave the era the name of Taika, meaning "Great Change," placed all land under the charge of the emperor, who had the sole right to redistribute it. This effectively abolished the hereditary right of local chieftains to apportion land. From a permanent capital and provincial divisions would emanate the nation's political stability, permanent institutions of government, central control over the provinces and a certain disrespect for the traditional Shintō taboo against maintaining a palace polluted by the death of an emperor. From taxation would come revenues for emperors and bureaucrats, the labor needed to build large palaces and government buildings and the concept of equality among imperial subjects. The Taika Reform installed unequivocally the imperial government as the source of all authority and marked the abolition of local autonomy.

Following the Taika Reform, a new administration was appointed in 702. At its highest level, the government consisted of the Great Council of State and the Department of Religion. Under these were two ministers of state, the Minister of the Left and the Minister of the Right, who controlled eight ministries: the Central Office, and the Ministries of Ceremonies, Civil Affairs, Popular Affairs, War and Justice, the Treasury and the Imperial Household. The latter two have survived until the present. That the Department of Religion should be at the new government's highest level is to be expected. This department regulated Shintō by ranking its shrines, and by extension its deities, much as the emperor ranked members of the new bureaucracy. Thus the emperor became not only Japan's sole landowner but also an authority superior even to the local divinities. An important reorganization of Shintō was to come out of this office, as we shall see later.

Another of Emperor Tenchi's innovations when he was still Crown Prince was the building of a water clock. Water clocks originated in China where they were first built sometime during the Latter Han Dynasty (A.D. 25-220). This extremely complicated yet ingenious device accurately measured the passing of time by water flowing down tanks arranged in a step-like formation. The level of water in the lowest tank indicated the time of the day. The water clock was installed in a building in Asuka, the foundation of which has only recently been excavated, and the hours of the day announced by the sounding of a bell. It was a device of a highly political significance intended to imbue the people with a new sense of time and order. The leaders of the day were convinced that a regulated sense of time would enable their control over the people.

With these reforms and innovations, the Japanese leaders tried to adopt the symmetrical and orderly Chinese system of government. It should be pointed out, however, that many of the institutions Japan imported from China were not suited to Japanese conditions and had to be adapted considerably. The Chinese examination and merit system, for example, which was the core of their civil service, was never fully accepted in Japan; on the contrary, clan chieftains were appointed as nobles and bureaucrats until civil servants and the aristocracy

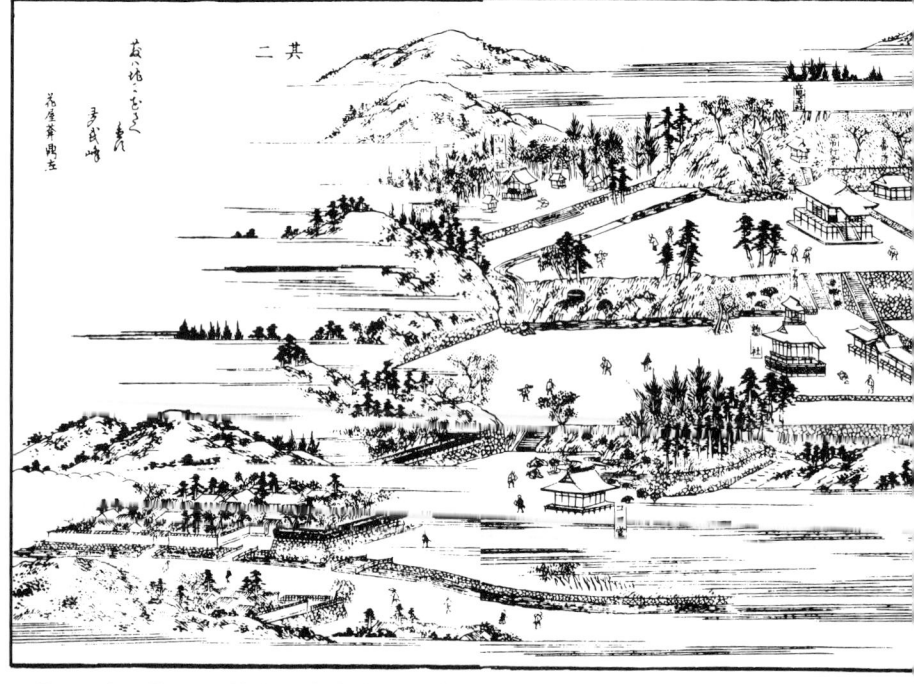

Tōnomine, Tanzan Shrine (*Saikoku Meisho-zue*)

eventually became one and the same. The Taika Reform also failed in some respects due to inequalities in the tax system as, for example, the emperors liberally distributed tax free land to aristocrats and temples for services rendered. Inequalities also forced small families to give their land to large families unable to meet their tax requirements. Unwittingly, the reformers tended to preserve the status quo under a new system.

In the long run, these reforms did alter the Japanese state; they firmly rooted the principle of a centralized nation administered by the emperor which, though not always adhered to in Japanese history, has remained a significant political ideal often sought after and emulated

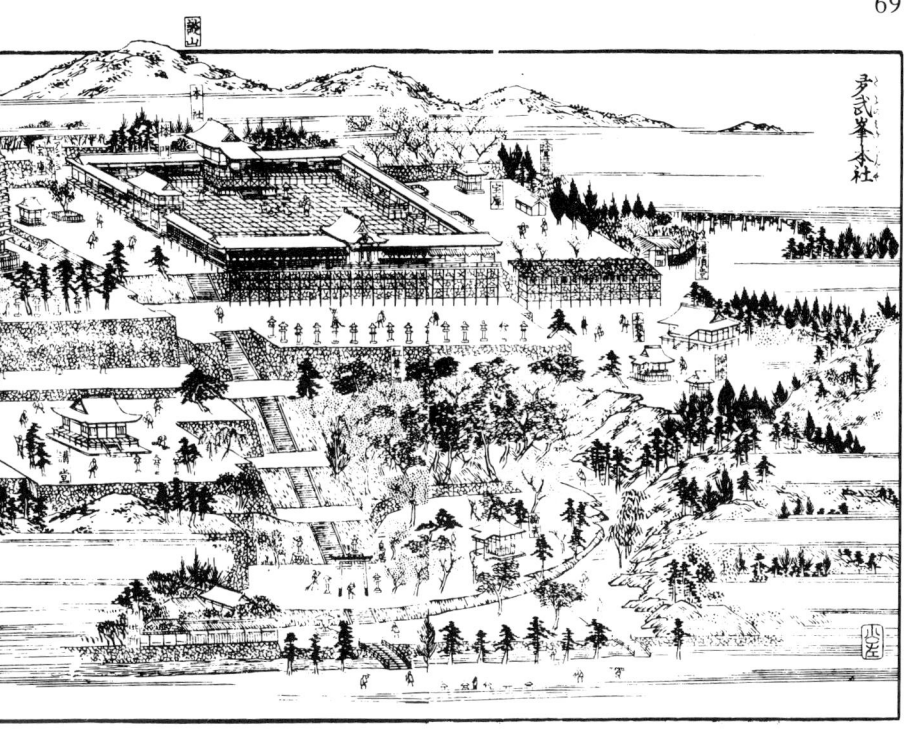

by later generations of Japanese statesmen quite until recently.

Tanzan Shrine: This shrine in the southern hills of the Yamato Plain was installed when the remains of Fujiwara no Kamatari were brought here by his son, Priest Jōe. One reason why this particular site was selected was that Kamatari apparently planned his coup of 645 here. The choice might also have been prompted by the beauty of the hills of Mt. Tōnomine from which one has a panoramic view of the entire Yamato Plain. The soul of Kamatari permanently laid to rest here could watch over and protect the plain. Indeed, the mountain is alleged to have groaned whenever the emperor or the Fujiwara were in danger. These groaning noises were reported to the court a total of thirty-six times in the course of history, whereupon special prayers were promptly ordered.

When Kamatari's grave was transferred to Tanzan Shrine, Priest Jōe installed a thirteen-storied pagoda in the grounds of the neighboring Myōraku-ji Temple as an expression of Fujiwara policy to promote the merger of Buddhism and Shintō. Up until the early Meiji Period (1868-1912), both temple and shrine were merged on Mt. Tōnomine.

Tanzan Shrine was destroyed several times by war and the caprices of nature. It was restored in 1451 with funds from the flourishing Japan-China trade. The greatest damage was inflicted in the Meiji Period when, due to the policy of separating Buddhism and Shintō in order to purify the latter from foreign influence, many of the temple halls were destroyed or dismantled. All but the pagoda at Myōraku-ji were demolished. This picturesque thirteen-storied pagoda, all of its thirteen roofs thatched with crypress bark, is an Important Cultural Property and remains the symbol of Tanzan Shrine.

Each year in the afternoon of the second Sunday in November, a match of imperial football (players kick the ball to each other all the while trying to keep it in the air for as long as possible) is played and a scroll displayed depicting the historic meeting between Kamatari and Prince Naka no Ōe that led to the overthrow of the Soga clan. A statue of Kamatari sculpted and installed in the Honden (Main Hall) in the eighth century is still there today.

FUJIWARA, THE FIRST "PERMANENT" CAPITAL

Kamatari's son, Fujiwara no Fubito (659-720), continued to carry out the directives of the Taika Reform, and it was under his direction that the first "permanent" capital was founded. To accommodate the growing bureaucracy, Emperor Temmu (r.672-686) sent a messenger in 684 to divine an appropriate setting for a permanent site. The site revealed was ideal. It was surrounded by the Three Mountains of Yamato (Mt. Miminashi in the north, Mt. Unebi to the west and Mt. Amanokagu to the east) in the Asuka region. Temmu did not live to see the capital but died in 686; it was Empress Jitō (r.686-697) who, shortly after her accession to the throne, made the final decision after inspecting the site accompanied by a retinue of one hundred officials. In order to prepare the land a ceremony was held to placate the indigenous local deities in 692 and messengers were sent to four shrines, including Ise, the ancestral shrine of the imperial family dedicated to the sun goddess Amaterasu (Heaven Shining Deity) from whom the family claimed descent, to report the building of the new capital to their respective deities. The land was then distributed among members of the imperial and other prominent families.

As part of a Shintō ritual to inaugurate the new capital, called Fujiwara, poems of praise were composed. The following is an example:

On the Well at the Palace of Fujiwara.

Our great Sovereign who rules in peace,
Offspring of the Bright One on high,
Has begun to build her Palace
On the plain of Fujii,
And standing on the dyke of Lake Haniyasu
She looks around her:
The green hill of Kagu of Yamato
Stands at the eastern gate,
A luxuriant spring-time hill;
Unebi, with its fragrant slopes,
Rises at the western gate,

72

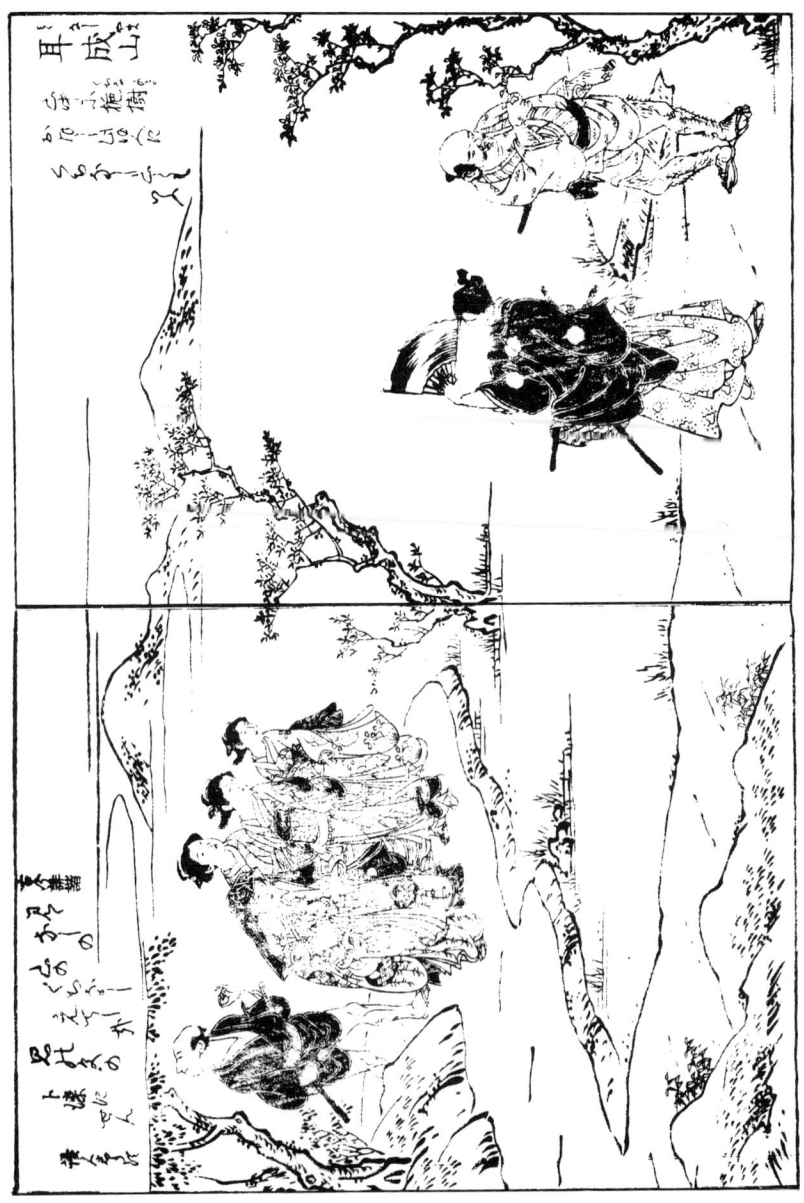

Mt. Miminashi (*Yamato Meisho-zue*)

Ever fresh and flourishing;
Miminashi, the green sedgy mount
Rears at the northern gate
Its form divine;
And the mountains of Yoshinu, of lovely name,
Soar into the sky,
Far from the southern gate.
At this towering Palace,
The shelter from the sun,
The shelter from the sky,
The waters will be everlasting,
These clear waters of the sacred well!

(Manyōshū)

Because of the magical power words, and especially names were believed to possess, these poems in praise of the land were employed to appease the local deities, and so prepare the site for imperial occupation. Their function was similar to that of the poems composed during the ''looking-down-over-the-land'' ritual.

Easy communication was vital to the well-being of the new state, both as a means to centrally control near and distant provinces and for the flow of taxes from the country outside the perimeters of the Yamato Plain to support the growing central bureaucracy. Consequently Fujiwara's road network was a particularly important factor in its selection as capital. Its most southerly east-west street, Ku-jō or Ninth Street, was, in fact, an extension of Kamitsu Road which afforded communication with the country north of the Yamato Plain. The northernmost road was the Yoko Ōji which extended from Naniwa (present-day Osaka) to Ise and eastern Japan. Fujiwara's easternmost road was a continuation of Shimotsu Road which lead over low passes to Yoshino and the Kii Peninsula in the south and to Tamba and the Japan Sea to the north of the Yamato Plain. These roads probably dated back about 100 years to the reigns of Emperors

74

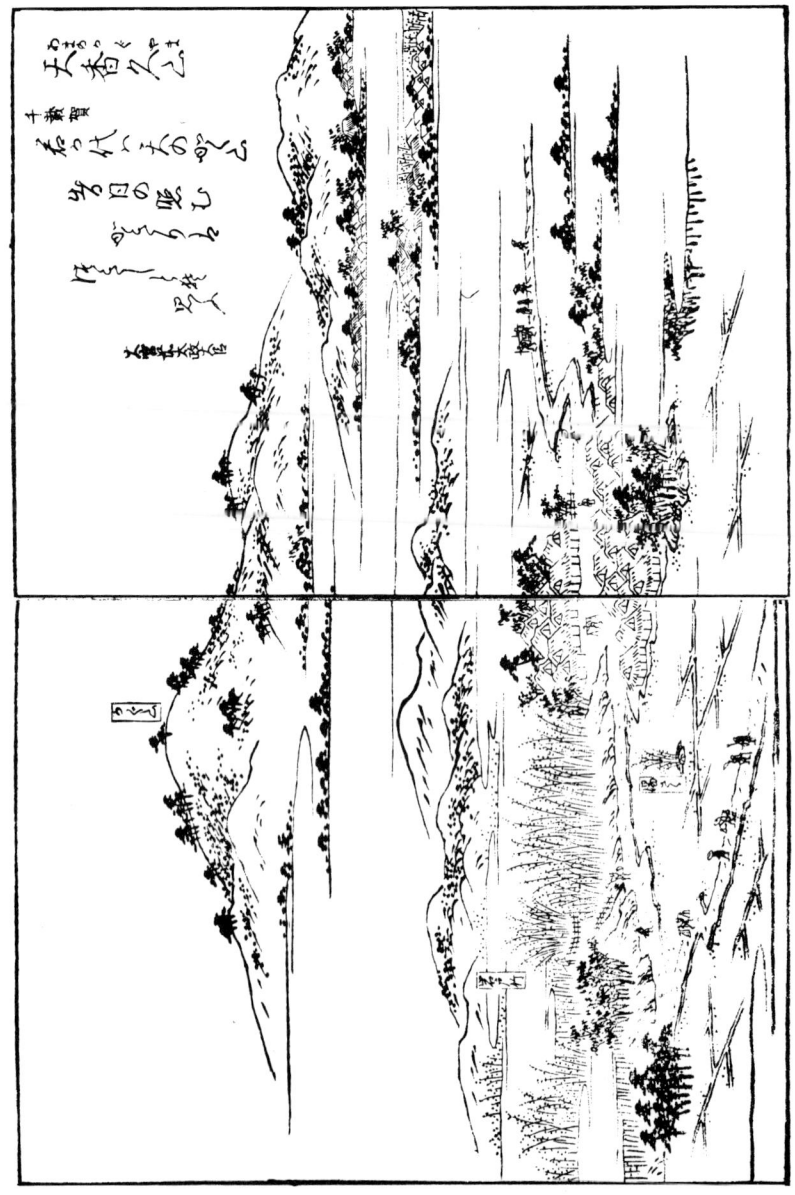

Mt. Amanokagu *(Yamato Meisho-zue)*

Yōmei and Bidatsu. The Yoko Ōji's link with Naniwa was particularly valuable for that was the port through which Japanese ambassadors proceeded to China, and through which Chinese and Koreans entered when travelling to Yamato. Naniwa was also the gateway to Western Honshū, Shikoku and Kyūshū.

The model for the new capital appears to have been the city of Lo Yang when it was capital during the Northern Wei Dynasty (386-534). It was arranged according to the rules of Chinese political and administrative symmetry. Fujiwara was divided into two equal halves by the Suzaku Ōji, the main avenue, which ran from north to south. Twelve east-west and nine north-south streets intersected to form blocks of equal size. Fujiwara was the first Japanese capital to be laid out in the grid plan known as *jōri*.

The imperial enclosure was situated in the center of the northern part of the capital, its northern extremity slightly below Ni-jō or Second Street. In the southern end of the enclosure was a large compound called Chōdō-in (Morning Audience Hall). The twelve pavilions it was divided into included the Eight Ministries, and halls for the ministers and imperial princes. The Morning Audience Hall (so named because government work was generally conducted in the morning) was surrounded by a wall with gates at its south and north ends. The northern gate led into the Daigoku-den (Great Hall of State), reserved for imperial audiences, which was itself surrounded by yet another wall with a gate to the north which opened on to the actual palace. All these gates aligned with the Suzaku Ōji, which continued past the city gate in a southerly direction toward Emperor Temmu's grave.

A number of temples were built in the new capital and others were transferred from elsewhere. Yakushi-ji Temple and Umayasaka-dera Temple were built in the eastern half and Daikandai-ji Temple in the western segment. These were later transferred to Nara (where Umayasaka-dera became the famous Kōfuku-ji Temple) and will be discussed in the context of Nara temples.

THE FUJIWARA AND NARA(HEIJŌ)CAPITALS

KITANOBE

NARA(HEIJŌ)CAPITAL

ICHIJŌ(FIRST)STREET

FORMER PALACE

LATER PALACE

NIJŌ(SECOND)STREET

SANJŌ(THIRD)STREET

MIBU GATE
SUZAKU GATE

GAIKYŌ
(OUTER CAPITAL)

SHIJŌ(FOURTH)STREET

SAKYŌ
(LEFT CAPITAL)

UKYŌ(RIGHT CAPITAL)
GOJŌ(FIFTH)STREET

ROKUJŌ(SIXTH)STREET

SHICHIJŌ(SEVENTH)STREET

HACHIJŌ(EIGHTH)STREET

KUJŌ(NINTH)STREET

NAKATSU ROAD

*YONBŌ
(FOURTH BLOCK)*

*SANBŌ
(THIRD BLOCK)*

*NIBŌ
(SECOND BLOCK)*

*ICHIBŌ
(FIRST BLOCK)*

SHIMOTSU ROAD

MT.
MIMINASHI

YOKO ŌJI ROAD

KAMITSU ROAD

FUJIWARA
CAPITAL

ICHI-JŌ

NI-JŌ

SAN-JŌ

SHI-JŌ

GO-JŌ

ROKU-JŌ

MT. AMANOKAGU

SHICHI-JŌ

HACHI-JŌ

MT. UNEBI

KU-JŌ

JŪ-JŌ

JŪICHI-JŌ

JŪNI-JŌ

YON-BŌ

SAN-BŌ

NI-BŌ

ICHI-BŌ

TO EMPEROR TEMMU
AND EMPRESS JITŌ'S
TOMBS

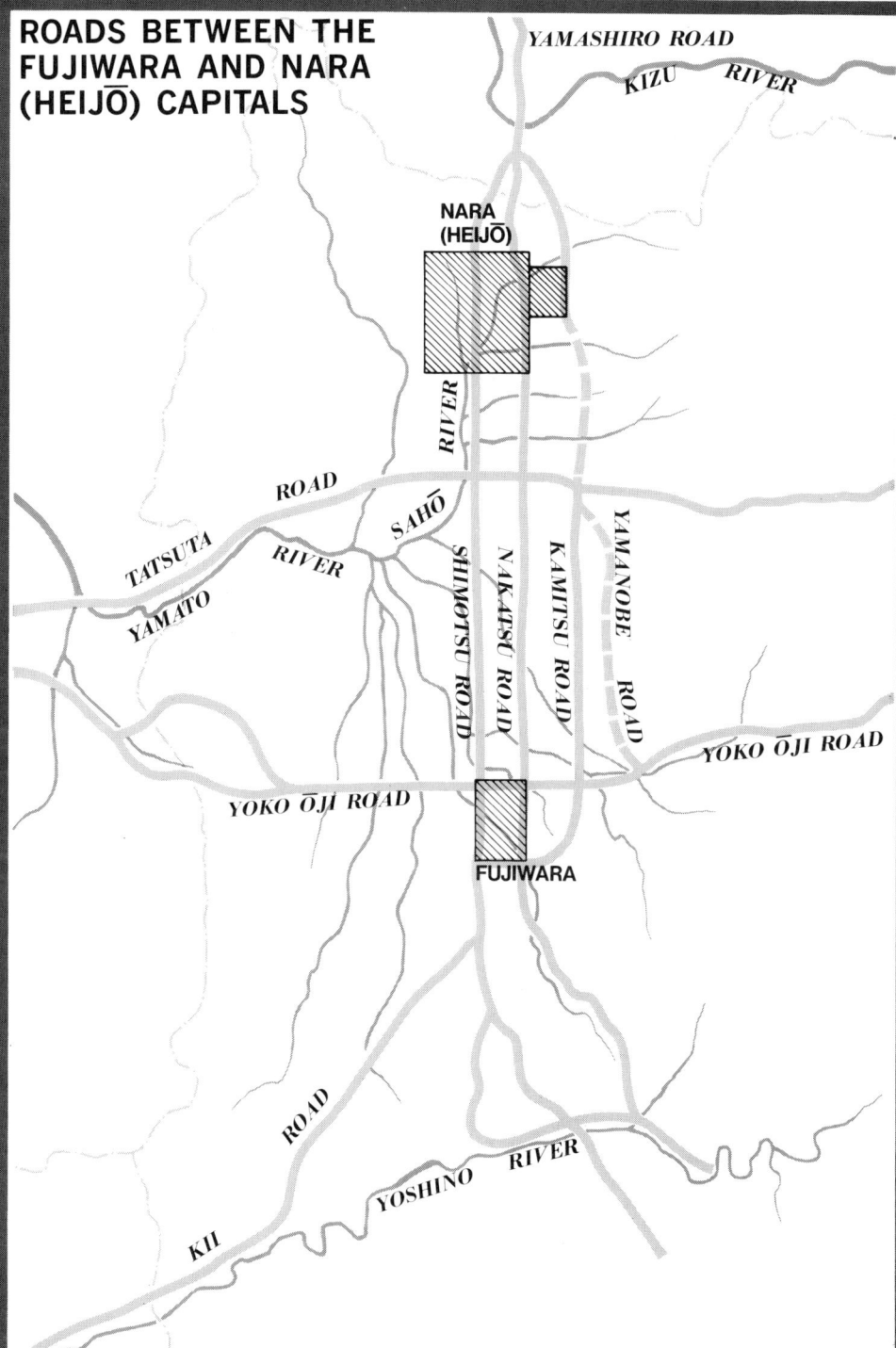

ROADS BETWEEN THE FUJIWARA AND NARA (HEIJŌ) CAPITALS

YAMASHIRO ROAD

KIZU RIVER

NARA (HEIJŌ)

RIVER

TATSUTA ROAD

YAMATO RIVER

SAHŌ

SHIMOTSU ROAD

NAKATSU ROAD

KAMITSU ROAD

YAMANOBE ROAD

YOKO ŌJI ROAD

YOKO ŌJI ROAD

FUJIWARA

ROAD

YOSHINO RIVER

KII

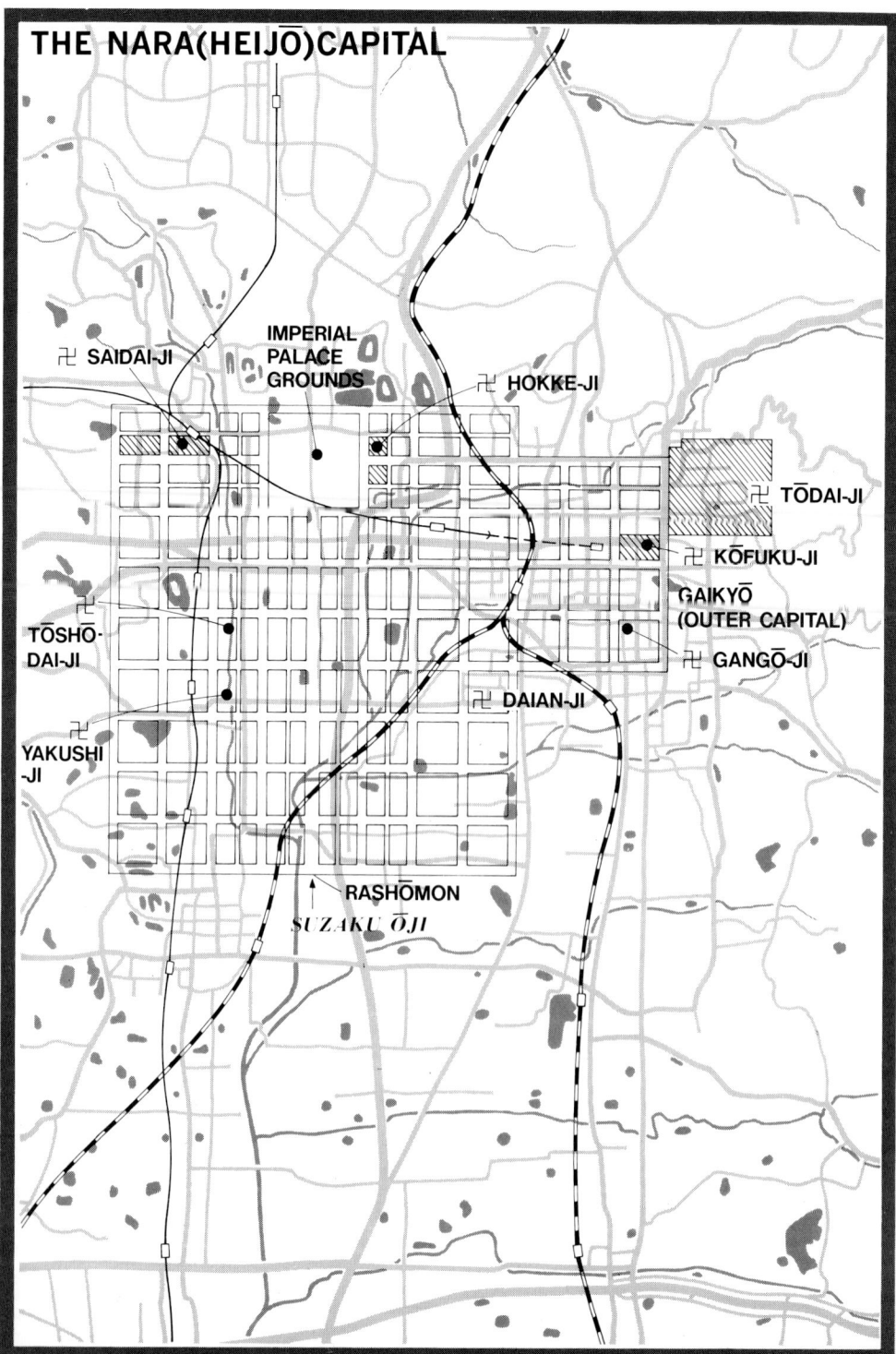

THE NARA(HEIJŌ)CAPITAL

卍 SAIDAI-JI

IMPERIAL
PALACE
GROUNDS

卍 HOKKE-JI

卍 TŌDAI-JI

卍 KŌFUKU-JI

TŌSHO-
DAI-JI

GAIKYŌ
(OUTER CAPITAL)

卍 GANGŌ-JI

卍 DAIAN-JI

YAKUSHI
-JI

RASHŌMON

SUZAKU ŌJI

NARA

The Imperial City of fairest Nara
Glows now at the height of beauty,
Like brilliant flowers in bloom!

Ono no Oyu *(Manyōshū)*

A mere fifteen years after the "permanent" capital was established at
Fujiwara, it was decided to relocate yet again, this time to Nara. The
reasons why Fujiwara was abandoned after only two emperors had
resided there are to be found in the political milieu of the period. The
Fujiwara, under the leadership of Fubito, planned to consolidate their
power by eventually enthroning Fubito's grandson, Prince Obito
(later Emperor Shōmu, r.724-749). A move to Nara it was thought
would facilitate Obito's accession. In addition the Fujiwara capital was
proving too small for the growing bureaucracy and also Nara offered
more efficient and natural communication with areas outside the
Yamato Plain — an important feature, given the emphasis of
communication and the policy of bringing distant areas of Japan under
central control.

And so in 708 Empress Gemmyō (r. 707-715) declared: "The area
of Heijō [the official name for Nara] conforms with the laws of
geomancy, three mountains protect it and the result of the divination
was good. The capital must be built here." The site complied with the
geomantic prerequisites of "Air and Water," Chinese principles for

determining the site of a capital: namely that the site must be enclosed in the north, east and west by mountains, it must be served by a number of rivers, and a pond, the symbol of central power, should be located in the south.

After the selection of the Nara capital had been reported to the Ise Shrine, the land was made level — it being inauspicious to carry out political affairs on sloping ground — even to the extent that two imperial tombs were removed to make way for the palace buildings. In 709, however, the superintendent for construction was ordered to restore the tombs because the emperor and high ministers considered it inauspicious to live upon a leveled tomb.

The new capital was to be triple the size of Fujiwara, a rectangular 4.8 kilometers by 4.3 kilometers. Reflecting Chinese political symmetry, the capital was divided by the central north-south avenue into separately administered right (western) and left (eastern) halves. These provided the basis for the nation's division into the western and eastern provinces. There were nine (the highest single-digit odd number) east-west streets and nine north-south streets, forming eight (the highest single-digit even number) blocks at each level, 71 in all.

The imperial enclosure was located in the northern extremity of the capital. In Fujiwara, two streets had lain between the northern edge of the palace and that of the city. The structure and disposition of pavilions within the enclosure followed by and large the pattern of Fujiwara. By the reign of Emperor Shōmu, however, the Chōdō-in, Daigoku-den and a new imperial palace had been relocated slightly to the east of the original palace, destroying the symmetry of the capital. This may have been an attempt to enthrone Emperor Shōmu in an unpolluted area in conformity with the old Shintō taboo. The new eastern palace was accessible by the Mibu Gate and the older building by the Suzaku Gate, beyond which the Suzaku Ōji, the main avenue, ran south in the direction of the Rashō-mon, the city gate of huge proportions.

The street system of Fujiwara which lay about 16 km. to the south of Nara was a particularly important consideration in the selection and lay-out of the new capital. Fujiwara's easternmost road, Nakatsu Road, extended to the north eventually becoming Nara's easternmost street. Fujiwara's westernmost road extended north to Nara's Rashō-mon where it linked up with Suzaku Ōji. The road at the southern extremity of Fujiwara, the Kamitsu, made a 90 degree turn towards the north then reached to Nara where it flanked the eastern edge of a 12 block addition to the capital called the Gaikyō, or Outer Capital.

Thousands of laborers were forced to leave their home provinces to work in the construction of the new capital, partly because of the new system of corvée labor instituted by the Taika Reform. A number of documents describe the severe hardships, hunger and starvation many of these laborers endured. Several poems written at this time refer to people who died by the roadsides; this happened probably because the food supply system had collapsed and there had not been enough for the laborers to eat on their way home. Here is an example taken from the *Manyōshū*.

> *Seeing a dead body lying among the*
> *stones on the island of Saminé*
> *in the province of Sanuki [Shikoku]*

> O SANUKI of beautiful seaweed
> On which I never tire to look!
> So fair is the province
> Because of its origin,
> And so hallowed the land
> For its divinity,
> With the very face of a god
> Enduring full and perfect
> With heaven and earth, with sun and moon.

I, travelling from place to place,
Embarked at Naka's haven
And thence sailed on,
When with the tide the wind arose,
Blowing from the dwelling-place of clouds.
I saw the billows racing on the sea,
And white surges beat upon the shore.
In fear of the whale-haunted sea
We rowed, straining the oars,

And sought, of all the islands thereabout,
Saminé, the island of renown,
And on its rugged coast
We built a hut for shelter.

There I found you, poor man! —
Outstretched on the beach,
On this rough bed of stones,
Amid the busy voices of the waves.

If I but knew where was your home,
I would go and tell;
If your wife but knew,
She would come to tend you.
She, knowing not even the way hither,
Must wait, must ever wait,
Restlessly hoping for your return —
Your dear wife — alas!

ENVOYS

Had your wife been with you,

She would have gathered food for you —
Starworts on Sami's hill-side —
But now is not their season past?

On the rugged beach
Where the waves come surging in from sea
You sleep, O luckless man,
Your head among the stones!

NARA TEMPLES AND SHRINES

Were it not for the endorsement of Buddhism, it is highly probable
that the Taika Reforms would not have been possible. It is therefore
not surprising that a close parallelism between the state and Buddhism
was sought, or that many temples were built in Nara as a physical
demonstration of the intimate relationship between the two. In
addition to the new temples, many others were transferred from
Fujiwara to the new capital. More than fifty pagodas are said to have
adorned Nara's skyline at one time. Victims of time, political and
natural upheavals, many have disappeared until only eight of the most
important temples remain today.

Nara's past is intimately linked with these surviving temples,
each of which transmits in its own way a fragment of Nara's history.
Tōdai-ji expresses the relationship between Buddhism and the new
state and the cultural achievements of the Nara Period; Tōshōdai-ji
bespeaks the close bond that existed between Japan and China; the
Yakushi-ji marks the development of the Japanese writing system; and
the Kōfuku-ji is a reminder of the ascendancy of the Fujiwara clan and
its role in the nation's political and cultural evolution. Each temple also
reveals the enormous cultural achievements of this period in the arts

and architecture. By visiting in addition the numerous temples built outside the capital during the Nara Period, one becomes freshly aware of the extent to which Nara's influence reached into every corner of the Yamato Plain and eventually to distant parts of the entire country. In spite of the brevity of the period, which lasted, including some temporary relocations of the capital, from 710 to 784, it was nevertheless the cornerstone of a nation unified under a central authority. The period also saw Japan firmly ensconced as one of the great artistic nations of the world.

Kōfuku-ji Temple: The origins of the Kōfuku-ji can be traced back to Nakatomi (Fujiwara) no Kamatari who, in order to secure victory over the rival Soga clan, vowed in 645 to donate a Shaka Triad and Four Heavenly Kings to Shitennō-ji Temple. He died before the statues were finished, and as a result they were not given to the Shitennō-ji but were installed instead in a private chapel established in Kamatari's memory at his former residence. When the capital was relocated in Fujiwara the statues too were transferred and a larger temple, called Umayasaka-dera, raised to house them. When the site of the capital was changed to Nara, the statues were moved once again and the temple, renamed Kōfuku-ji, or Bestowing Happiness Temple, found a permanent home overlooking the capital from the lower slopes of the eastern mountain. The statues were installed in the Chūkondō (Central Main Hall).

Kōfuku-ji was initially the family temple of the Fujiwara. In honor of Fujiwara no Fubito, in 721, on the first anniversary of his death, it was declared an official temple and as such a place where prayers for the well-being of the state and health of the emperor were offered. In memory of Fubito, Empress Genshō (r. 715-724) and ex-Empress Gemmyō donated the Hokuendō (North Circular Hall). As a rule, temples had two pagodas, but Hokuendō was built where one of these was to have been erected. That Fubito should thus replace the Buddha Shaka, symbolized in the pagoda, is a phenomenon that may be explained by the importance of ancestor worship in Japan's native religion. Octagonal halls, it should be noted, were often built as memorial chapels in Japanese temples. Hokuendō contained statues of Miroku, his attendant bodhisattvas and two disciples of Shaka.

Over the next few years a number of halls were added. The construction of the Tōkondō (East Main Hall) was ordered in 726 by Emperor Shōmu as a votive prayer for the recovery of ex-Empress Genshō. A five-storied pagoda was added in 730; Empress Kōmyō, Fubito's daughter and wife of Emperor Shōmu, was most probably its patron. The five stories symbolize the Five Elements — wood, fire, earth, metal and water — and the nine rings circling the steeple, the nine spheres of heaven. In memory of Lady Tachibana, Empress Kōmyō's mother, the Seikondō (West Main Hall) was added in 734 on the first anniversary of her death. Its sacred statues included a Shaka attended by two bodhisattvas, ten disciples of Buddha and, fashioned from dry lacquer, the Hachi Busshū (Eight Demon Guardians of Buddhism) which are now in the Treasury. Apart from the bird-faced Karura and the bearded Hibakara, the other Busshū — Gobujō, Ashura, Kuhanda, Shakatsura, Kinnara and Kendatsura — all have gentle, almost childlike countenances. The head of Shakatsura is crowned with a snake, Kinnara's with a unicorn's head, Kendatsura's with a lion's face and Gobujō's with a unidentifiable animal's head. About ten years after the building of the Seikondō, the Kōdō (Lecture Hall) and Shikidō (Refectory) were probably completed.

The Tōin (China Hall) was built as a repository for the five thousand theological volumes brought back from China in 735 by the priest Gembō which became the basic texts of the Hossō School of Buddhism. Priest Gembō had spent 19 years in China studying Hossō and Chinese culture prior to becoming Kōfuku-ji's first Head Priest. The Tōin was jointly sponsored by the four branches of the Fujiwara family descended from Fubito. Fuyutsugu of the leading northern branch of the clan built the Nanendō (South Circular Hall) in 813 bringing to an end the construction of Kōfuku-ji Temple. A

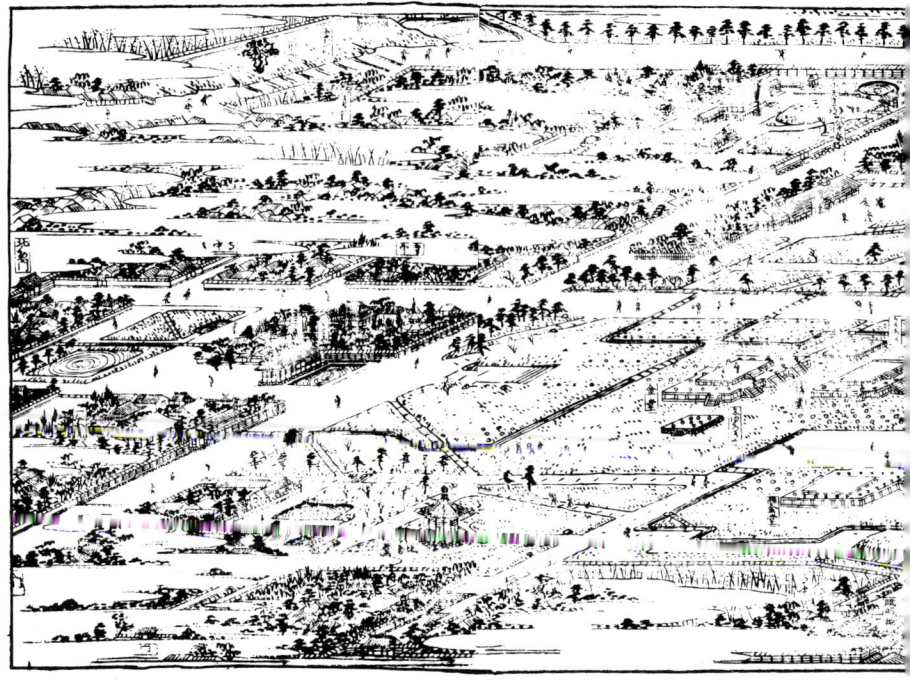

Kōfuku-ji Temple and Sarusawa Pond *(Yamato Meisho-zue)*

Fukūkenjaku, the Kannon who brings those submerged in the murky waters of illusion to the shore of Truth, was taken from the Kōdō to be Nanendō's central figure of worship.

Six schools of Buddhism were established during the Nara Period: Hossō, Sanron, Jōjitsu, Kusha, Ritsu and Kegon. These were not sects per se but teachings based on particular scriptures or aspects of Buddhism. As the teachings did not differ greatly, it was not unusual in some temples for priests to study more than one. The Hossō School claimed all phenomena to be mere illusions, creations of the mind. The moon was neither beautiful nor sad, merely "as it is." Realizing the true nature of the universe, the school taught, would lead to enlightenment, for which all mankind has the potential but which can

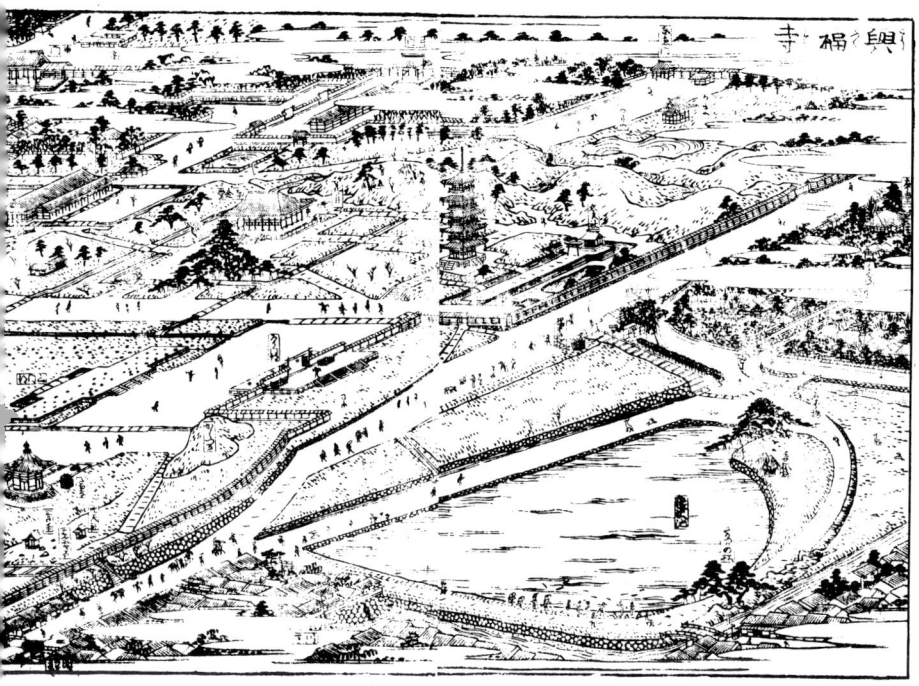

only be attained with practice. In spite of scholarly speculations about the essence of life, Nara Buddhism was essentially this-worldly. Prayers were made for the protection of the state, recovery from illness and fortune in war, all of which are reflected in the history of the Kōfuku-ji Temple and its various halls.

Buddhism and Shintō were gradually amalgamated. In 937, a Kōfuku-ji monk by the name of Shōen declared that the Shintō deity of Kasuga, the Fujiwara ancestral deity, had appeared to him in a dream in the form of a merciful bodhisattva expressing a wish to become the protector of Kōfuku-ji Temple. Ten years later, probably due to the support the Fujiwara, originally Shintō ritualists, gave to the synthesis of the two religions, Kōfuku-ji monks performed a Buddhist ceremony at Kasuga Shrine inaugurating the merger of temple and shrine. Two pagodas were erected to mark the road between Kōfuku-ji and Kasuga.

Kōfuku-ji fell prey to fire several times in its long history. In the fire of 1046, only two of its buildings escaped the flames. It was rebuilt according to the original plans but there were further fires in 1060 and 1096. The greatest devastation occurred in the conflagration of 1180 when two rival military clans, the Taira and the Minamoto (similar to the Ōtomo and Mononobe of pre-Nara days), were competing for supremacy at a time when the puissance of the Fujiwara aristocracy was on the wane. Taira no Shigehira, fearing that Kōfuku-ji's monk-army* might ally against him, razed the entire complex. There was no time to carry all the statues to safety and many of them were consumed by the flames.

Rebuilding efforts began almost immediately but were not completed for another 60 years. The lost statues were replaced with new ones carved by famous Kamakura Period (1185-1333) artists, who applied to them the realism typical of the new, feudal era which had departed from the idealistic aristocratic values and aestheticism of the Heian Period. The Kōfuku-ji employed these artisans on a hereditary basis. They and their descendants lived and worked in the temple and were on occasion commissioned to other temples. Many masterpieces of Japanese art came out of Kōfuku-ji's busy workshops. The sculptor Kōkei (dates unknown) carved the gold-surfaced wooden Fukūkenjaku Kannon that is the main object of worship in the Nanendō (South Circular Hall) as well as the wildly ferocious Four Heavenly Kings on exhibit in the same hall. His son Unkei carved the statues of Miroku and the two Indian theologians, Muchaku (Asanga)

---

* The central government had lost control over the provinces by the end of the Heian Period causing temples to entertain their own armies in order to control their provincial land holdings on which they depended for their revenue.

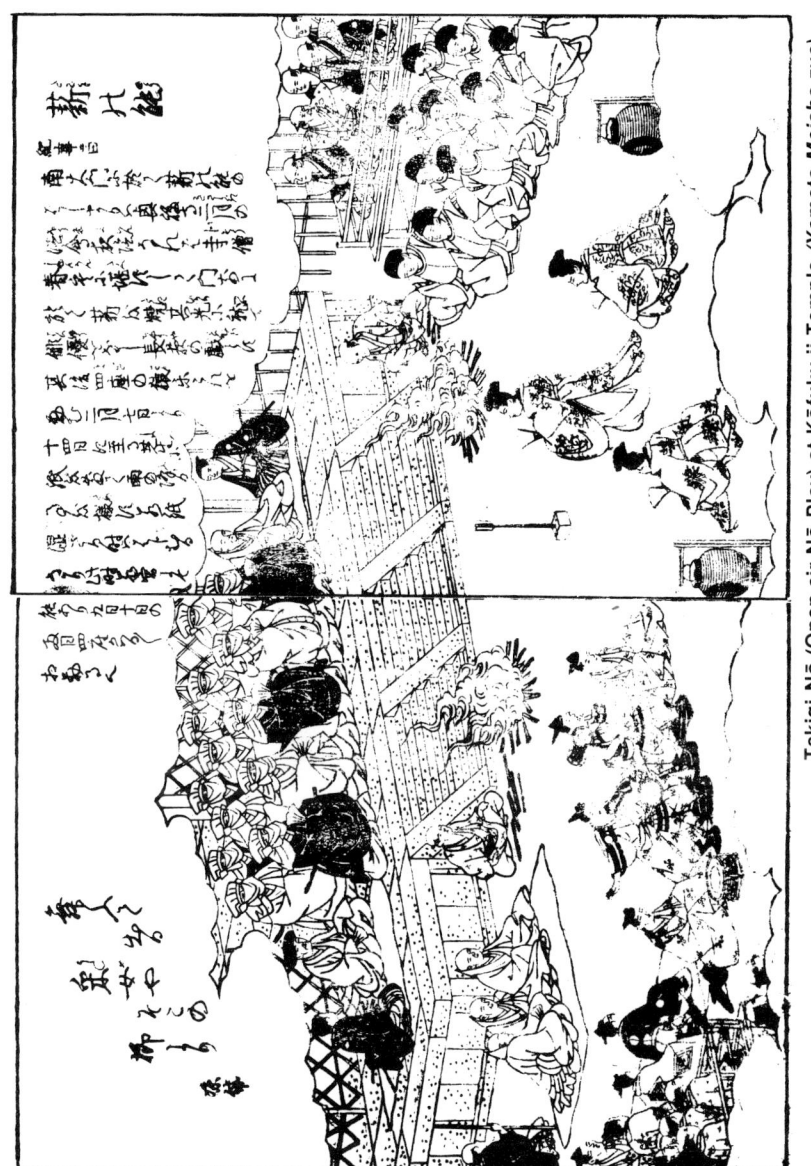

Takigi Nō (Open-air Nō Play) at Kōfuku-ji Temple (*Yamato Meisho-zue*)

Takigi (Open-air) Nō Play at Kōfuku-ji Temple (*Nō no Zushiki*)

and Seishin (Vasubandhu), from whose teachings the Hossō School developed, all of which can still be worshipped in the North Circular Hall. The renowned sculptor Jōkei (thought to be Unkei's second son) carved the Yuima which stands now in the Kokuhōkan (Treasury). The story of Yuima (Vimalakirti), one of Buddha's disciples, is recounted in the *Yuima-kyō* Sutra which is recited annually on October 10th in a formal ceremony at the Kōfuku-ji. The very wealthy Yuima helped the poor and was respected as a model Buddhist citizen. Jōkei is probably also responsible for the two statues of the Kongō Rikishi (fierce looking protectors of the Buddhist law) which kept guard at the Seikondō until that building burned down. They are now to be found in the Kokuhōkan Treasury. Kōben, Unkei's third son, created the lantern carrying demons, Tantōki and Ryūtōki, also once displayed in the Seikondō but now in the Treasury.

Kōfuku-ji Temple's days of glory did not last and it was destined to suffer as much from neglect and adverse political developments as from conflagrations. It never recovered from a fire in 1717 after which only a few of its buildings were restored. The military rulers of the Edo Period (1600-1868) were not disposed to support a temple originated by the Fujiwara aristocrats, who had by that time become insignificant. Kōfuku-ji received no better treatment at the hands of the Meiji government. During that period State Shintō based on the divinity of the emperor was emphasized, and consequently Japanese Buddhism as a whole suffered. In 1868, the Kasuga Shrine severed its ties with Kōfuku-ji Temple and became independent. Three years later the Meiji government appropriated some of the temple buildings; the Central Main Hall became the Nara Prefectural Office and the Refectory was converted into a public school. All their valuable statues were squeezed into the Northern and Southern Circular Halls. In 1881 much of Kōfuku-ji land was converted into a public park. Fortunately, the government realized the artistic value of the temple's statuary and decided to build the Kokuhōkan Treasury in which to exhibit them. In order to gather sufficient funds for the construction of the Treasury the government allowed members of the public, for a few coins, to climb the five-hundred year old pagoda, the oldest extant Kōfuku-ji building dating from a reconstruction in 1426.

The Treasury was completed in 1958. The statues on display here include most of those which once stood in the various Kōfuku-ji Temple halls. Also here is a masterpiece of Japanese sculpture, the famous statue of Ashura, one of the Hachi Busshū. Ashuras, believed to be evil deities in Brahmanism, were looked to by the Buddhists as protectors of the faith. This particular statue portrays a demon who having been tamed by Buddhist saints serves as a protector of Buddhism. Its six graceful arms denote the Ashura's supernatural powers to keep all evil at bay, and its delicate facial features are gentle and human-like. Even the most ferocious demons show compassion and kindness to those who conquer the evil illusions of their hearts.

Gangō-ji Temple: Gangō-ji is the name given to Asuka-dera Temple when it was transferred to Fujiwara at the time of the capital's relocation there. In 680, it was designated as an official temple. Gangō-ji became associated in particular with the Sanron School of Buddhism brought to Japan in 625 by the Korean monk Ekan. Very little is known about Ekan, or for that matter about any of the early priests, but we do know that he resided at Asuka-dera and that on one occasion in 646 he was invited to give a lecture at the court on Sanron teachings. Sanron is based on the Three Treatise of Nagarjuna, the distinguished Indian monk and Buddhist theologian responsible for developing Mahayana Buddhism. Sanron teachings claim that everything in the universe is impermanent and void of substance and that the ultimate principle of truth underlying all phenomena can only be understood by paradox and not by rational means. Sanron teachings were later absorbed by Tōdai-ji which eventually became the head temple of the school.

Because Gangō-ji had been a Soga temple originally, the Fujiwara resisted its transfer to Nara. Finally, in 718, land was set aside for the

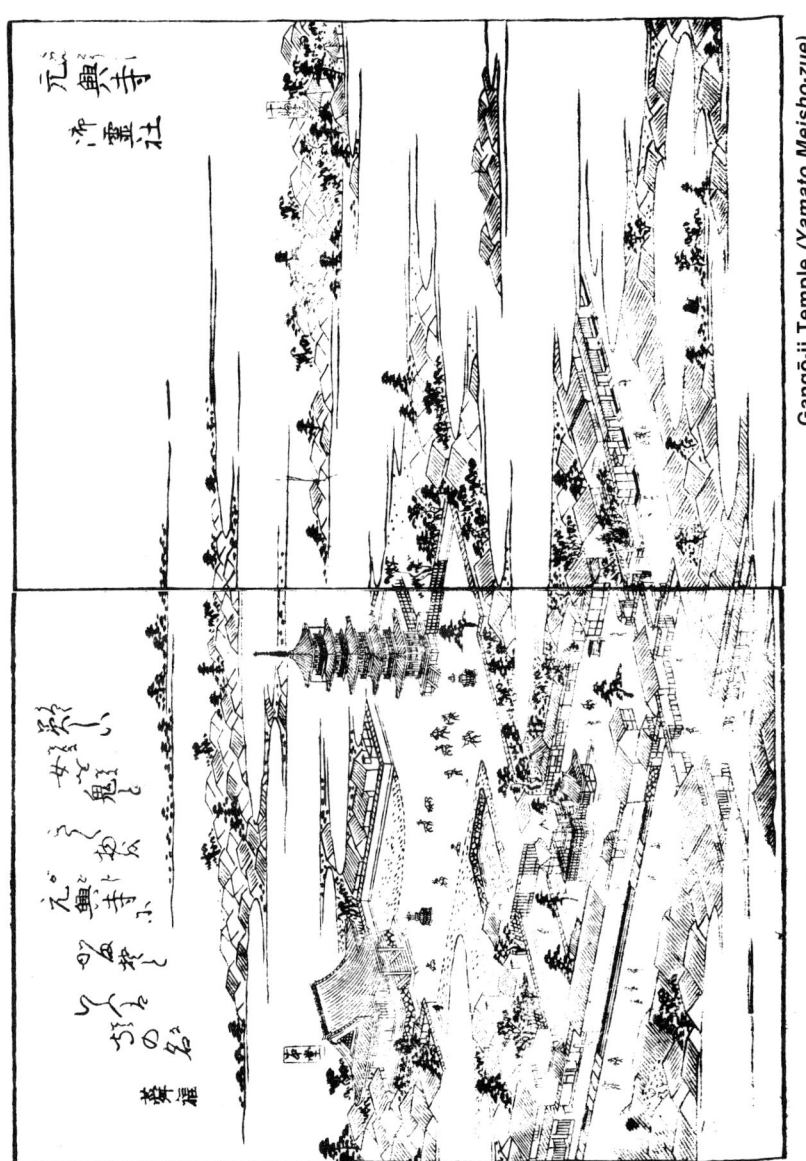

Gangō-ji Temple (Yamato Meisho-zue)

temple in the new capital where it gained status by being declared an official temple and by being endowed with land in the provinces for its subsistence. The Kondō (Main Hall) was located in the very center of the temple grounds and beyond it the Kōdō (Lecture Hall). The Main Hall was surrounded by a cloister that converged in the north at the Lecture Hall and in the south at the Chūmon (Middle Gate). To the north of the Lecture Hall in a north-south arrangement stood the Belfry and the Shikidō (Refectory). An enclosure entered by either the Hokumon (North Gate) or the Nandaimon (South Great Gate) encircled these buildings. Outside the cloister, between the Middle and the South Great Gates, were two pagodas: the smaller Shōtō-in to the west and the large Daitō-in to the east. All that remains today of the original Gangō-ji is part of its priestly quarters, remodeled in the Kamakura Period and renamed Zendō (Zen Hall). National Treasure, it measures 26.6m in length and 6.6m in width.

Although Gangō-ji lost its standing to the Tōdai-ji as the center of Sanron Buddhism, by the end of the Heian Period (794-1185) it had become the core of Jōdo (Pure Land) Buddhism, the sect based on the Buddha Amida's vow to save all those believing in him. Gangō-ji had in its possession a mandala portraying Amida in the "Pure Land," his Western Paradise, surrounded by his ever-present two attendants and additional 23 bodhisattvas. This mandala was painted on wood by one Priest Chikō (709-between 770 and 780) after he saw a vision of the Pure Land in a dream. In the dream he was directed to abandon scholarship and to rely on faith in Amida alone. Chikō's quarters were thenceforth called Gokuraku-bō (Paradise Quarters) and eventually became a separate, and also the most prosperous, unit of Gangō-ji Temple. All that remains of the Gokuraku-bō today is the Main Hall, a National Treasure dating from the Kamakura Period. A Kamakura Period replica of the Pure Land Mandala can be seen here.

Another National Treasure also dating from the Kamakura Period is the Main Hall of Jūrin-in Temple. It was once a part of Gangō-ji but became independent when Gangō-ji fell into disrepair following the transferral of the capital to Heian-kyō (now Kyoto) in 794. In the northeastern corner of Jūrin-in is a mound called Uokai-zuka which, according to legend, is the burial place of a child fathered in China by a Japanese ambassador. When the ambassador returned to Japan, the child followed his father by crossing the sea on the back of a fish. The child was a prodigious calligrapher and allegedly taught Kūkai (posth. Kōbō Daishi), the inventor of the Japanese *kana* syllabary, the art of writing.

Daian-ji Temple: The Daian-ji is another distinguished Nara temple only the name of which has survived. When Tōdai-ji (East Great) Temple and Saidai-ji (West Great) Temple were built, the Daian-ji became known also as Nandai-ji (South Great) Temple. Its roots reach back to Prince Shōtoku and the Buddhist seminary he built in 617 in Kumagori. Under Emperor Jomei, it was removed to the Kudara River area and renamed Kudaradai-ji (Kudara Great) Temple. In 674, the seminary was resituated again in Asuka and in 678 renamed Daikandai-ji Temple. In the seventh and eighth centuries it was the most important of all the official temples reserved for prayers for the state. When Nara became the capital it was transferred a third time, this time to Roku-jō (Sixth Street) where it assumed the name of Daian-ji (Great Peace) Temple.

Like Gangō-ji, it was arranged along the lines of a Chinese temple, with pagodas to the east and west of the inner temple ground, that was accessible by the Nandaimon (South Great Gate) and the Chūmon (Middle Gate). Unlike Gangō-ji, the Middle Gate was linked directly to the Kondō (Main Hall) and not to the Kōdō (Lecture Hall) which, like the Shikidō (Refectory) lay to the north of the Main Hall. By this arrangement, one could see the Main Hall immediately after entering through the Middle Gate, at the other end of a large courtyard surrounded by the cloister. Priestly quarters lined up with the complex to the east and west. Built four years prior to the Gangō-ji, Daian-ji was probably the first temple laid out in this style. It too

caught fire frequently; it was damaged in 949, 1017 and 1041 but was
rebuilt each time. Like Gangō-ji, it fell into disrepair after the capital
was transferred to Heian-kyō and was placed under the supervision of
Saidai-ji Temple. Daian-ji suffered further destruction in the
earthquake of 1449, and early seventeenth century documents record
only one hall there at that time. The present Main Hall was built in
1882 at the request of Saidai-ji.

Although none of the original Daian-ji buildings have survived,
nine of its late Nara Period statues have. They were fashioned using a
new style in which a statue was carved from a single block of wood
resulting in heavier, broader-shouldered and stabler looking figures.
This style was introduced to Japan by the priest Ganjin, for whom
Tōshōdai-ji was built, and first developed at that temple. The famous
Shitennō (Four Heavenly Kings), Senju (Thousand-handed),
Fukūkenjaku, Jūichimen (Eleven-headed), Yōryū, Shō and Datō
(Horse-headed) Kannon are good examples of the new style that
attempted to bring new life into Tempyō Period (729-794) art, which
had become stale and uninnovative. (Kannon bodhisattva can appear in
33 different shapes in order to save mankind. Among them, Shō
Kannon represents the bodhisattva in its original, yet untransformed
shape. Batō (Horse-headed) Kannon, originally a horse-headed Hindu
deity, has lost its horse-shaped head and assumed a human face in
Buddhism. To indicate its origin, the bodhisattva is often represented
with a small horse head crowning its own head. He is believed to
swallow the sins of men. The bodhisattva Yōryū, who holds a branch
of a willow, is a magician able to dilute the power of all poison.)

Hokke-ji Temple: Hokke-ji (also Hokkemetsuzai-ji or Lotus Sin
Forgiveness Temple) is a nunnery built in 745 in the grounds of
Empress Kōmyō's residence which her father, Fujiwara no Fubito,
had bequeathed to her. It consisted of East and West Pagodas, a
Kondō (Main Hall), Kōdō (Lecture Hall), Shikidō (Refectory), Kyōzō
(Sutra Repository), Belfry, Amida Jōdo-in Hall, Chūmon (Middle

Gate) and Nandaimon (South Great Gate) all symmetrically laid out. The Amida Jōdo-in Hall was built at the special request of the Empress and had as its main object of worship an intriguing Jūichimen (Eleven-headed) Kannon, the largest statue of its kind in Japan. The lotus leaves emanating from behind the statue to form its halo make it an unusual piece of art. The eleven heads represent the different facial emotions the Kannon assume when they come to earth to save lost souls. Each of this particular statue's faces are said to be carved in the likeness of the Empress.

There is a legend behind the faces of the statue. A king of India wanted very much to see a living bodhisattva and was led by a dream to go to Japan to see Empress Kōmyō. Reluctant to travel so far from his kingdom, he sent in his place a sculptor to carve a statue in her exact likeness. After many mishaps along the way, the sculptor finally arrived in Japan and was able to catch a fleeting glimpse of the Empress standing beside a pond. From this brief impression, he carved two statues of the Eleven-headed Kannon, one of which he took back with him to India. The truth of this story is unverifiable, but this Nara Period statue is one of only two religious relics to survive the stresses of time to which the Hokke-ji has been subjected during the past twelve centuries.

Following the death of her husband, ex-Emperor Shōmu, in 756, Empress Kōmyō became a nun and secluded herself in the Hokke-ji until she died four years later. When she fell ill, prayers for her recovery were held at the nunnery and the people forbidden to kill animals or eat their flesh. Buddhist law forbade the eating of animal flesh but although the priests complied with this prohibition the general populace often did not. In order to ensure the success of the supplications for the Empress' recovery, the law was temporarily enforced.

Hokke-ji's Hondō (Main Hall) possesses another outstanding statue in Yuima (Vimalakirti) that probably dates back to Yuima-e, ceremonies initiated by Fujiwara no Fubito in honour of Yuima. This

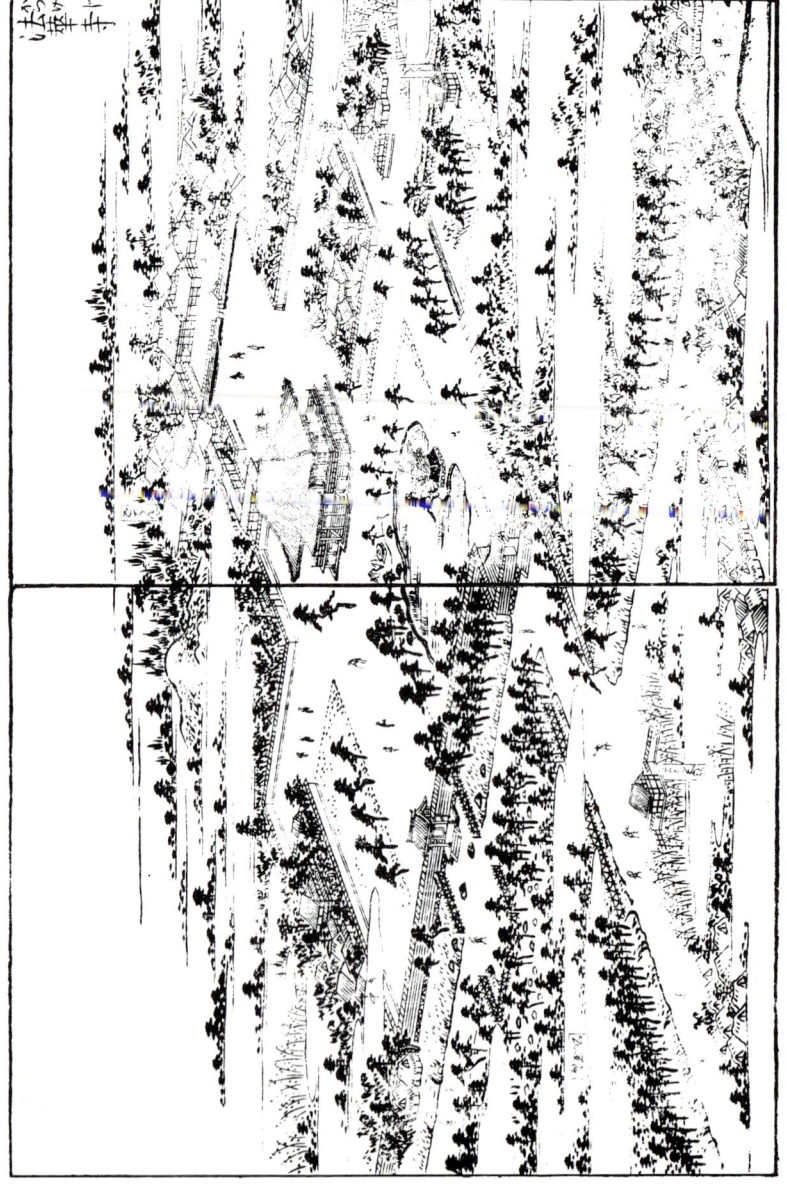

Hokke-ji Temple *(Yamato Meisho-zue)*

is a remarkable piece of latter Nara Period art.

In the Yokobuedō is a small statue made in the likeness of the girl Yokobue out of letters she wrote expressing her determination to abandon the world and retire to Hokke-ji. According to the *Heike Monogatari* (Tales of the Heike), written sometime in the thirteenth century, the Taira clan warrior Takiguchi fell in love with Yokobue, a maid of low rank, but his father strongly opposed the match. Takiguchi then decided to seek a religious life and secluded himself in a temple. After a painstaking search, Yokobue found her lover's whereabouts but it was too late. Acolyte Takiguchi was determined to stay away from the secular world. Realizing that her plea was hopeless, Yokobue too renounced the world and retired to Hokke-ji. Hearing of her decision, Takiguchi sent Yokobue a poem:

> Till you shaved your head
> And vowed to renounce the world
> Your heart found no peace.
> Surely you must now be glad
> Having entered Buddha's way.

To this Yokobue answered:

> Now I've shaved my head
> And became a cloistered nun,
> What should I regret?
> There can be no looking back
> Having entered Buddha's way.

(Transl. by A.L. Sadler.)

Hokke-ji too was designated as an official temple and when nunneries were built in each province in the country in 741, it was proclaimed their head temple. This brings us to one of the most important events in Nara Period history: the erection of Tōdai-ji

Temple and the consolidation of the parallelism between state and
Buddhism.

Tōdai-ji Temple: The building of Tōdai-ji Temple and the casting of
the famed Daibutsu (Great Buddha) which smiles benevolently in the
temple grounds are two of the most significant events of the Nara
Period, significant because they indicate the dramatic revolution that
was taking place in Japan's political and cultural mentality. The
Tōdai-ji and the Great Buddha were a direct outcome of Japan's
fascination with the powerful T'ang Dynasty in the seventh and
eighth centuries and her desire to discover China's secrets of success.
When the troops Japan sent to Korea in 663 to protect her ally
Paekché were crushed by the superior united Silla and T'ang forces,
Japan was overawed by and curious as to the strength of China. Only
two years later, she sent a mission to China seeking to re-establish
diplomatic relations; it was followed by many others over the
succeeding years as Japan eagerly sought to learn from and emulate
China's political and cultural achievements.

While investigating the reasons behind the success of the T'ang
Dynasty, the close link between Buddhism and the state and the
important role that religion played in uniting the people under one
faith must quickly have become apparent to the Japanese. The China
of the T'ang was conducted according to the precept that the state
must conform to the strict symmetrical order of the Buddhist
universe, thereby securing Buddhism as a state-supporting and
protecting official religion. Temples and government offices were
built side by side indicating that the emperor, his government and
military officials were the earthly counterparts of Buddhas, their
attendant bodhisattvas and the ferocious protecting deities of the faith.

Although Tōdai-ji Temple reflected Japan's wish to adopt the
Chinese parallelism between state and Buddhism, it was also a
response to more immediate problems. The early Nara Period was
pervaded with political strife. In 740 a rebellion instigated by Fujiwara

no Hirotsugu forced Emperor Shōmu to flee Nara for Kuni, then to Shigaraki and finally, in 743, to Naniwa. It was at Shigaraki that the first attempts were made to cast a giant Buddha in the hope this would unite the people and restore much needed amity to the nation. Shōmu must have heard of China's great Buddha in the outskirts of the capital Lo Yang, and also of Silla's intention to build a similar statue. The Shigaraki project failed and so did a second endeavor at Naniwa. Refusing to be discouraged the Emperor issued an edict to cast another great Buddha three months later. A large tract of land was flattened just north of Kōfuku-ji Temple where the Buddha was to be cast and a temple built to shelter it. Three experts in casting were appointed, and despite the complicated logistics, about four hundred tons of copper and tin were mined and transported to the site. This was an enormous investment for those days. Between 747 and 749 eight castings were attempted and numerous technical difficulties had to be overcome before a Buddha was finally cast that would not topple over.

A statue of such huge proportions was never before seen in Japan and must have made an awesome impression on all who looked upon it. The Buddha's face alone measured 5 meters across, the length of the palm was 3.7 meters and that of the middle finger two meters. Even the protrusion on top of its head was larger than a normal human head. The nostrils were large enough for a man to crawl into. Its lotus pedestal alone weighed one hundred and thirty tons. Standing sixteen meters high, it included 443,700 tons of copper, 41,160 tons of mercury, 81.6 tons of tin and a considerable quantity of gold. Japan had intended to import gold from China and Korea with which to coat the surface of the Buddha until in 749 the discovery of gold in the Province of Mutsu (roughly Iwate Prefecture) was reported. The discovery was interpreted as a sign of welcome by the native Shintō deities and a pledge to protect the Buddha.

Deeply grateful for the completion of the Buddha, the Emperor abdicated in favor of his daughter Kōken (r. 749-758) and took the vows of the Buddhist priesthood. With much pomp, a ceremony was

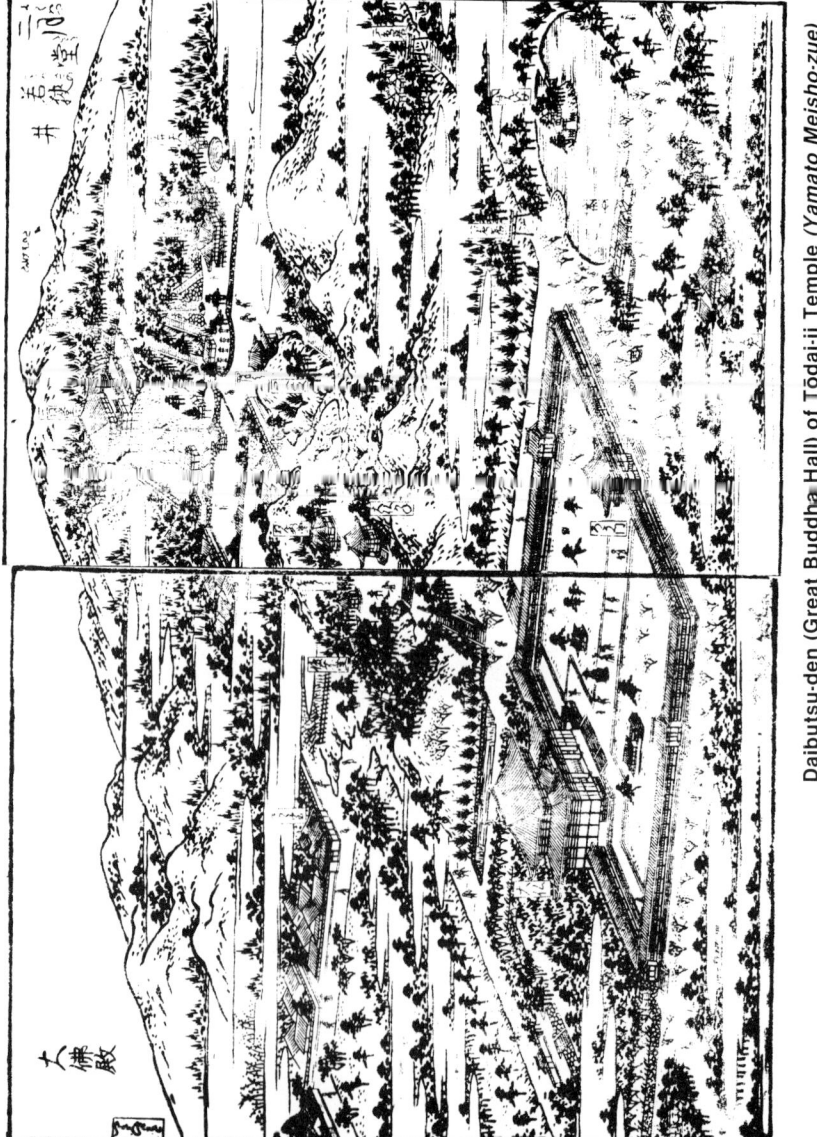

Daibutsu-den (Great Buddha Hall) of Tōdai-ji Temple (*Yamato Meisho-zue*)

GREAT BUDDHA, *Shigisan Engi Emaki*

GREAT BUDDHA, Tōdai-ji Temple

held to announce to the Great Buddha the discovery of gold. Ex-Emperor Shōmu proceeded in state to Tōdai-ji Temple where he stood facing north toward the Great Buddha, the position of a subject in audience with his sovereign. The Minister of the Left then advanced to announce to the Buddha, in the name of the ex-Emperor, the propitious finding.

Shortly afterwards, Shōmu fell seriously ill. Even though the gold had not yet been applied to the surface of the Great Buddha, or the Daibutsu-den (Great Buddha Hall) completed, preparations for the highly symbolic "eye-opening" ceremony were carried out in order that Shōmu be able to attend. On the day of the ceremony, in the year 752, Shōmu watched as his representative, the Indian monk Bodaisenna (Bodhisena, the first Indian to set foot in Japan), painted the eyes onto the Great Buddha, a symbolic awakening of the statue into life. He was assisted by Japanese and Chinese monks.

The casting of the Great Buddha was the last symbolic act in the centralization of the Japanese state. When Shōmu visited the Great Buddha in 749, to see the progress made in its construction, he had himself introduced to the Buddha as a "slave of the Buddhist religion," and he declared that ". . . the Great World of Buddha is the most excellent for protecting the state . . ." In so saying, Shōmu related himself and his state to the Buddhist universe. Like the Buddha at the center of the universe manifesting his will through various hierarchically subordinated Buddhas and bodhisattvas until it reached the world, the emperor was at the nucleus of the nation, extending his rule through high and low officials down to the last subject of the realm.

This merger of Buddhism and statecraft was further solidified by Shōmu's edict ordering sub-temples of the Tōdai-ji built in each province. In the same manner, as the emperor ruled over provinces via his appointed provincial governors, the head-priest of the Tōdai-ji had jurisdiction over the provincial sub-temples, each of which were called Kokubun-ji. With the casting of the Great Buddha, the emperor symbolically merged Buddhism and statecraft in a political and religious parallelism that was at the core of the new state's organization.

Shintō was not cast aside to make way for the joining of Buddhism and politics. The Emperor had already made it clear during his visit in 749 to the Great Buddha that he was not only the "Sovereign Prince of Yamato," but also "a Manifest God" ruling from the throne of "Heavenly Sun Succession." The discovery of gold making possible the Great Buddha's final coating was taken as a sign of the Shintō deities' pleasure with and acceptance of Buddhism in Japan. The Japanese may have found that the two religions were not incompatible. This realization led to the eventual synthesis of the two that would dominate the religious scene in Japan until the nineteenth century.

The first attempts to reconcile Buddhism and Shintō date from 742, a year before the emperor decreed the casting of a Great Buddha. A charismatic priest called Gyōgi is said to have represented the Emperor Shōmu on a journey to the great shrine of the sun goddess at Ise. He carried with him a Buddhist relic. Since the sun goddess was the ancestral deity of the imperial family, it is probable that the Emperor felt he needed to consult her about the matter of the Great Buddha. After Gyōgi had spent seven days and nights at the shrine in prayer the sun goddess spoke to him in Chinese saying that she welcomed the Buddha. Shortly afterwards, the goddess appeared to the emperor in a dream and proclaimed the sun and the Buddha to be one and the same. After this event, Buddhism and Shintō began to assimilate, and Shintō deities came to be regarded as incarnations or bodhisattva attendants of the Buddhas.

It took another thirty years after the successful casting of the Great Buddha to complete the entire Tōdai-ji Temple complex. The Daibutsuden (Great Buddha Hall) that contained the Great Buddha was an edifice of gigantic proportions designed to stress the strength of the Buddhism-state union. The original hall measured about 61

106

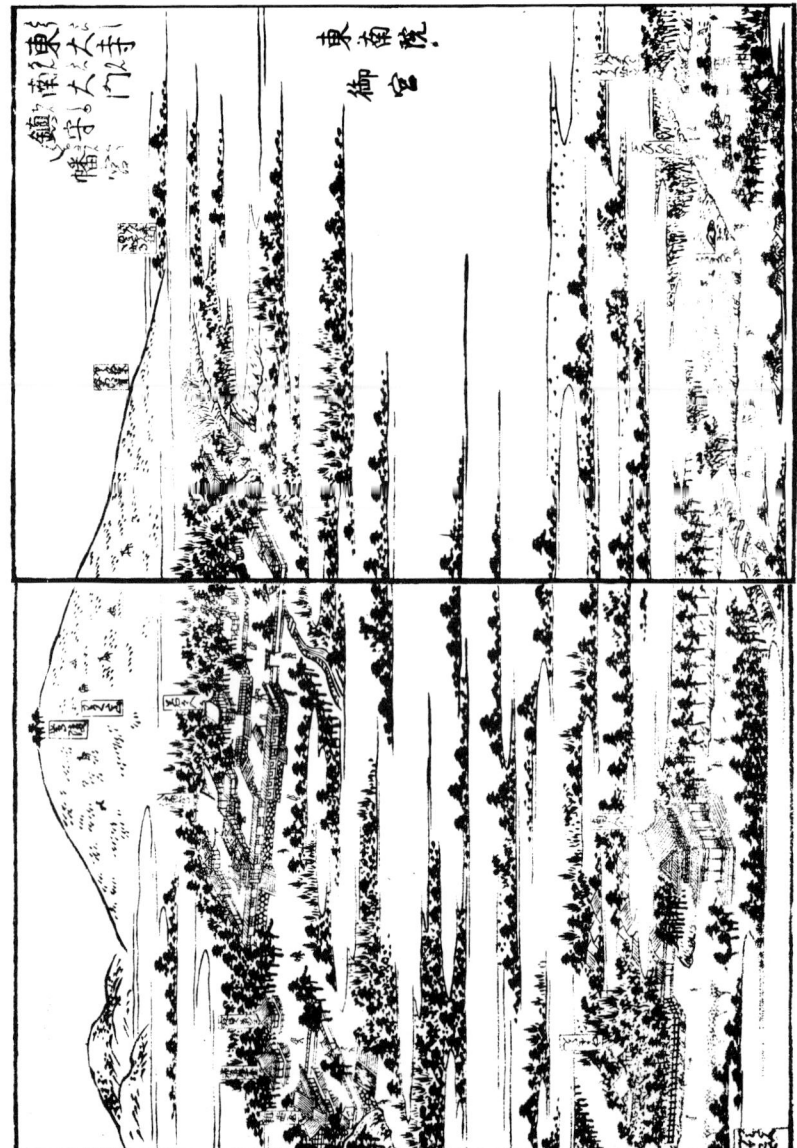

鎮守東大寺
八幡宮の南大門

東南院
御倉

Bottom: Nandaimon (South Great Gate) of Tōdai-ji Temple. Top: Hachiman-gū Shrine (*Yamato Meisho-zue*)

meters in height, twelve meters higher than the present-day structure, and its front length was one and a half times longer than it is today. Nevertheless, in spite of its reduced size, the present Great Buddha Hall, 57 meters long and 50 meters deep, is still the largest wooden structure in the world. The Hall was surrounded by a cloister and reached by proceeding through the Chūmon (Middle Gate). It lined up in a strictly north-south axis with the Kōdō (Lecture Hall) in the north and the Nandaimon (South Great Gate).

Two towering seven-storied pagodas, triple the height of the pagoda at Hōryūji Temple were erected between the Nandaimon and the Great Buddha Hall, one to the east and one to the west. Each was surrounded by a cloister, each one equal in area to the entire Hōryū-ji complex. The Kōdō was completed shortly after the eye-opening ceremony and a Monju and a Yuima statue as well as a Senju (Thousand-armed) Kannon attended by a Kokūzō and a Jizō installed. (Monju is one of the attendants of the Buddha Shaka incorporating the latter's wisdom. Kokūzō, holding the Sword of Wisdom in his left hand and the Lotus of Good Fortune in his right, bestows wisdom and good fortune. Jizō will teach and save people, especially children, from suffering until the advent of Miroku, the Buddha of the Future.) Priestly quarters and a Shikidō (Refectory) followed between 750 and 762.

The main gate at Tōdai-ji is the Nandaimon (South Great Gate). The original gate was about one third larger than the present gate's height of 25.5 meters. The Niō that stand guard at the gate are not quite as large as the original, which were consumed by fire in 1180, but are nevertheless of gigantic proportions. The Tengai (also Tegai)-mon (Revert Harm) Gate, located to the northwest of the Great Buddha Hall, was believed to cure passers-by instantly of any disease from which they might have suffered. It is a National Treasure dating back to the beginnings of Tōdai-ji.

The Kaidan-in (Ordination Hall) was built after the arrival in Japan of the Chinese priest Ganjin so that he could ordain priests in a

TAMON-TEN (above) and JIGOKU-TEN (left), two of the FOUR HEAVENLY KINGS, Kaidan-in, Tōdai-ji Temple

suitable setting. It houses the Shitennō (Four Heavenly Kings) made of dry clay, each one trampling upon a demon to demonstrate the subjugation of chaos and disorder. Each King has a different facial expression. Their power is not expressed in violent gestures but is interiorized by their serene postures. Their almost life-size dimensions point not only to a greater realism sought by artists at that time but also express the descent of Buddhist deities to the level of mankind.

The Hokkedō (Lotus Hall), built uphill and to the east of Great

JIGOKU-TEN

Buddha Hall in 733, is also known as Sangatsudō (Third Month Hall)
because of the reading here of the *Lotus Sutra* in March of each year.
The northern section of the hall may date back to a temple that existed
in the area prior to the erection of Tōdai-ji and which was
incorporated into the latter. This hall is akin to a museum today with
its numerous Buddhist statues clustered together in its far from
spacious interior room. The main statue may have been the
Fukūkenjaku Kannon that is still one of the most outstanding works

FUKŪKENJAKU KANNON,
Sangatsu-dō, Tōdai-ji Temple

of art on display in the Sangatsudō. The Kannon carries the rope with which he fishes or hunts for the souls of mankind. His six arms denote the Kannon's immense powers. Around his neck is an ornate necklace and on his head a silver crown adorned with an Amida in the middle and studded with thousands of pearls, agates and crystals, testimony to the vast wealth Buddhist temples had accumulated by the Nara Period. Also to be found here are the Four Heavenly Kings and a Nikkō (Sun) and a Gakkō (Moon) bodhisattva holding their hands together in prayer. Their faces overflow with piety. There are also a Benzai-ten and a Kichijō-ten, female deities of happiness and wisdom, both of which were in Tōdai-ji's Kichijōdō (Kichijō Hall) until it burnt down

NIKKŌ BOSATSU, Sangatsu-dō, Tōdai-ji Temple

in 954. Both deities were portrayed as extremely beautiful T'ang Dynasty court ladies again suggesting the closeness of Buddhist deities to mankind. Near the back door stands an angry-looking, dry clay Shukongō-jin (also Kongō Rikishi or Niō), a protector of Buddhism who with his diamond stick smashes all evil attempting to penetrate the Buddhist realm. It was initially secretly enshrined and hidden from both the public and the priesthood. This was not an uncommon practice. Except for special occasions statues were often concealed from worshippers, perhaps out of fear that constant exposure would diminish the deity's potency. Some statues are displayed only on certain occasions, others are classified as "zettai hibutsu (top secret)" and are never looked at, not even by the chief priests. The Shukongō-jin can only be viewed on December 16.

Near the Hokkedō stands the Nigatsudō (Second Month Hall), built as a prayer for the recovery of ex-Emperor Shōmu from an illness. Its name derives from a ritual called Shuni-e that has been performed in the second lunar month (now March) almost without interruption from 752 until today. Shuni-e is a form of collective confession. Eleven priests are selected annually to carry out this ritual (the festival itself is known as Mizutori) which they perform after first undergoing extensive purification. From March 1, from noon to midnight every day for two weeks, they perform a circumambulation around the altar of the Eleven-faced Kannon (a "zettai hibutsu" statue), who exonerates the sins of man, all the time reciting its name. This they do without drinking a drop of water. This is intended, according to one interpretation, to bring heaven and earth together by abolishing time. To atone for their sins, the participating priests fall on their knees in turn. On March 5 and 12, they recite at a fast tempo the names of almost two thousand Buddhist and Shinto deities and a list of all the sins people might have committed during the year. The ritual reaches its climax on the 11th and 12th when ten, huge burning torches are carried up to the verandah of Nigatsudō shaken by their bearers so that millions of sparks fly down upon the crowd symbolically burning away their sins.

The Shuni-e ritual is also interpreted as the burning away of winter to allow spring to arrive. That is why in the early morning hours of the 13th, the priests draw the first water of spring from a sacred well that is believed to connect with the area of Wakasa (now Fukui Prefecture). Spring has not arrived for the people of Nara until the Shuni-e has been observed.

The only structures to escape the fires and earthquakes the temple was subjected to were a group of buildings called the Shōsō-in (The Treasury). These were, ironically, the simplest of all Tōdai-ji's structures. In 756, in a ceremony marking the forty-ninth day of the death of ex-Emperor Shōmu, Empress Kōmyō donated his personal belongings to the Great Buddha as a votive prayer for her husband's soul. These were kept in the six log cabins that the Shōsō-in consisted of which, although deceptively simple in appearance from the outside, are proof of the ingeniousness of Nara Period builders. It was designed so that in humid weather the logs would expand permitting only a minimum of humidity to penetrate into the interior, and in dry weather they would shrink allowing fresh air to circulate inside. The floor was raised about three meters off the ground to prevent the accumulation of humidity underneath. It is thanks to this inventiveness that so many historical objects have been preserved all these hundreds of years.

The Shōsō-in was enriched by later donations. Among its treasures are the ritual implements used in the inauguration of Tōdai-ji. Today the Shōsō-in is an incomparable museum of Nara antiquities that include writing materials, musical instruments, clothing, ornaments, weapons, medicines and glass cups. Some of the items came from Korea, China and as far away as India and Persia, evidence of the richness of culture that travelled the Silk Road from the eastern Mediterranean and from India to Japan. Many of these items were gifts received by Japanese ambassadors from their Chinese hosts.

The octagonal gilt bronze lantern in front of the Great Buddha Hall is another vestige of the original Tōdai-ji. Its low relief is adorned with angelical musicians and lions, and its roof is crowned with a flaming heart. The cedar outside Nigatsudō is called Rōben Cedar because people believe that it was planted when Rōben was the first head-priest of Tōdai-ji. Rōben is also remembered with a statue, a National Treasure, in the Kaisandō (Founder's Hall).

With the exception of portions of the Great Buddha, parts of the Sangatsudō, the statues and the lantern, there are only a few of the original Nara Period buildings left at Tōdai-ji. All others are later reconstructions for Tōdai-ji too suffered at the hands of nature and

114

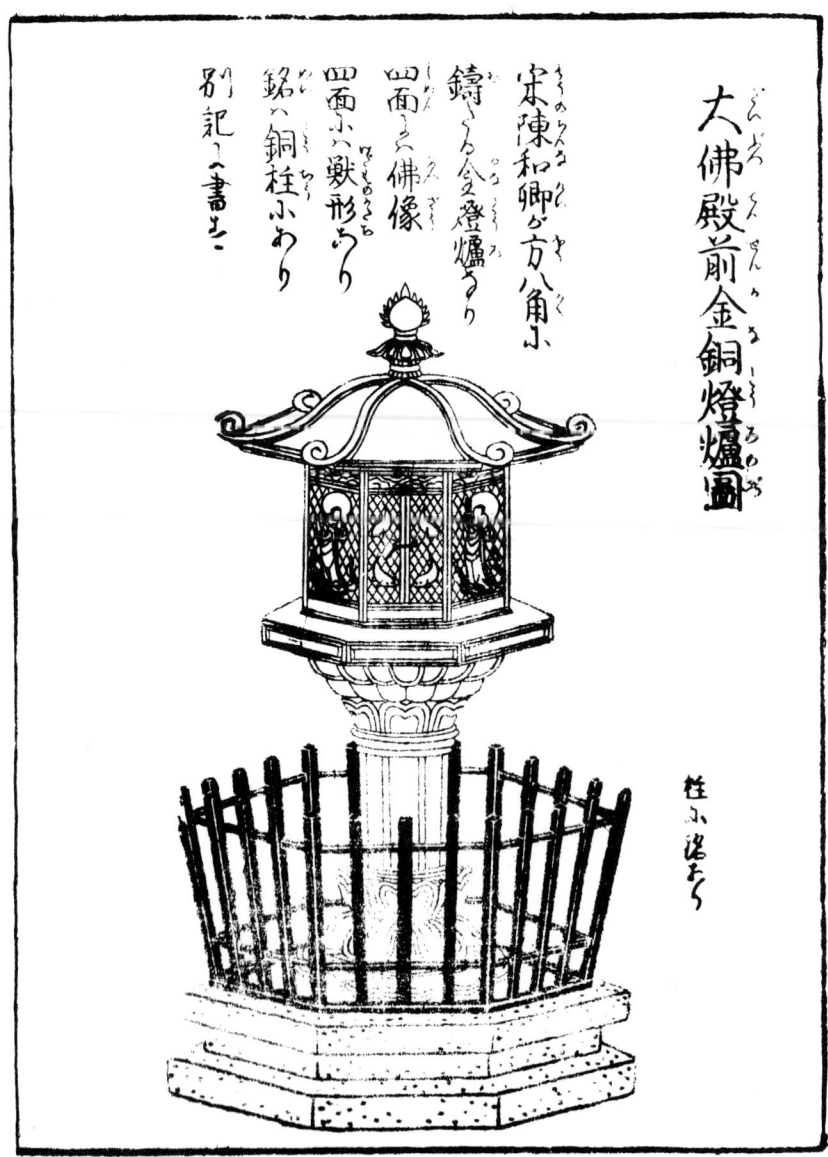

別記ニ書セリ
銘ハ銅柱ニアリ
四面ニ獣形アリ
四面ニ佛像
鋳タル金ノ燈爐ナリ
宋陳和卿ガ方八角ナ

柱ハ洛ナリ

大佛殿前金銅燈爐圖

Bronze Lantern, Tōdai-ji Temple *(Yamato Meisho-zue)*

political upheavals. In 786, the back of the Great Buddha split. About thirteen years later the right hand fell off and in 855 its head was shaken off by an earthquake. The statue was repaired in 861 and priests from the Yakushi-ji and Gangō-ji Temples assisted Tōdai-ji priests in the eye-opening ceremony of the restored Great Buddha. In 934, the Western Pagoda burnt down followed twenty years later by the Kichijōdō. The Eastern Pagoda too suffered damages on several occasions but was repaired in 1100.

The greatest destruction Tōdai-ji was to sustain came in 1180 when Taira no Shigehira razed the entire complex, except for Shōsō-in and part of the Hokkedō, during a raid of the Nara temples he suspected of siding against his clan. Much of the Great Buddha was probably melted by the heat emanating from the Great Buddha Hall as it went up in flames and only parts of its lotus pedestal remained.

Rebuilding the Tōdai-ji was a project of national proportions, the supervision of which was entrusted to the energetic Priest Chōgen (1186-1235) of Daigō-ji Temple. He had already visited China three times and brought back to Japan the vast knowledge he had gained there. Funds for the reconstruction came initially from the revenues of two provinces but when this proved insufficient, support was sought nationwide by the Kanjin (fund-collecting) priests. Much of it came from Kyoto aristocrats and from ex-Emperor Goshirakawa (d. 1192) himself. Minamoto no Yoritomo (1147-1199) took a personal interest in the temple's reconstruction since for him, as the first Shōgun of the Kamakura military government and victor in the conflict with the Taira clan, it was a prayer for the return of Japan to the peace and prosperity known in Shōmu's Nara. In 1181 the Great Buddha was recast with the assistance of a priest from Sung Dynasty, China and the eye-opening ceremony performed personally by ex-Emperor Goshirakawa. The Great Buddha Hall was rebuilt using a new technique imported from China and completed in 1195. At 49 meters high it was considerably smaller than the original hall. The Kamakura Period sculptors Unkei, Kaikei and Kōkei carved the Four

Heavenly Kings surrounding the Great Buddha, one in each of the four directions. The South Great Gate, 25 meters high, was also rebuilt on a reduced scale. Unkei and Kaikei assisted by 18 other sculptors, carved the colossal eight meter-high Niō Guardians at the Great South Gate using the multiple-block technique. Priest Chōgen, whose relentless efforts allowed for the reconstruction of Tōdai-ji, is worshipped in the Shunjō-dō Hall where a statue of him, a National Treasure of the Kamakura Period, is being preserved. This statue too belongs to the masterpieces of sculpture throughout the world.

Disaster struck Tōdai-ji yet again in 1567 when the Great Buddha Hall was destroyed during a civil war and the head of the Great Buddha once more toppled off. For the next 130 years, the Great Buddha was exposed to the elements. Finally Tokugawa Ieyasu (1542-1616), the first Shōgun of the Tokugawa Period and who established military headquarters in Edo (present-day Tokyo), sponsored the necessary repairs but these were not completed until 1691. The Tōdai-ji was never to regain its original splendor. The pagodas and a number of halls were never rebuilt. Considering the costs incurred in repairing just the Buddha and its hall, we should perhaps be grateful that they at least remain to remind us of the cultural splendor of the Nara Period.

Yakushi-ji Temple: When Empress Jitō became afflicted with an eye disease in 680, Emperor Temmu ordered the building of the Yakushi-ji in Fujiwara, the capital at the time, as a votive prayer for her recovery. The prayer was addressed to Yakushi, the Buddha of Healing, and one hundred men were ordered into the priesthood to serve the temple. When the Empress recovered, Temmu proclaimed a general amnesty. When shortly after he too fell ill, another hundred men were ordered to enter the priesthood to pray for him. Emperor Temmu did recover but died in 698, before the completion of the Yakushi-ji.

It is possible that the temple would never have been completed

were it not for the attempt to placate the embittered soul of Prince
Ōtsu, a victim of one of the many successional struggles. Prince Ōtsu,
one of Temmu's sons by another consort, had been next in line to the
throne, but Empress Jitō, who became ruler upon the death of her
husband, determined that her own son be crown prince and outlawed
Ōtsu forcing him to commit suicide. He was only 23 years old. When
Ōtsu's wife heard of her husband's death she ran barefoot to his grave
and killed herself there. Princess Ōku, Ōtsu's sister and priestess of the
Ise Shrine, composed this lament upon hearing of his tragic demise.

> From to-morrow ever
> Shall I regard as brother
> The twin-peaked mountain of Futagami [Nijō]—
> I, daughter of man.
> *(Manyōshū)*

The bitter souls of political victims such as the prince were very much
feared in ancient Japan, and it is possible that the expansion of the
Yakushi-ji might also have served the double purpose of placating
Ōtsu's revenge-seeking spirit.

Empress Jitō continued to sponsor the temple. In honor of its
inauguration, she donated an embroidery, which was carefully
preserved for over 800 years until it was consumed by fire in 1528. Jitō
must have been a devout Buddhist for she was the first Japanese
sovereign to be cremated in accordance with Buddhist custom.

The transfer of Yakushi-ji to Nara in 718 is still an issue of
scholarly dispute. Some scholars claim that the temple remained at
Fujiwara under the new name of Motoyakushi-ji (Original Yakushi-ji)
and that an entirely new building was constructed in Nara using the
original Yakushi-ji plans. Others assert that it was dismantled and
transported, piece by piece, from the old Fujiwara capital to its present
site in Nara. I am inclined toward the latter theory because when a
capital was transferred in ancient Japan buildings were often taken

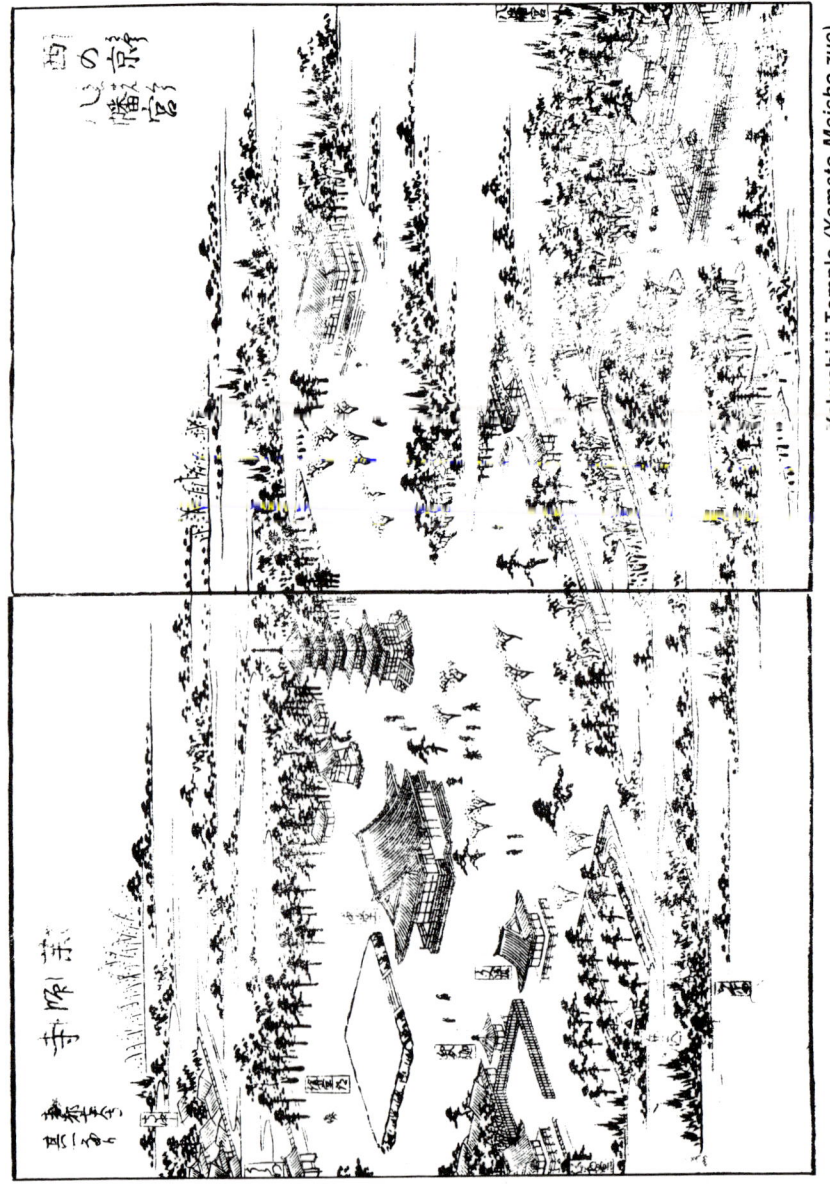

Yakushi-ji Temple (Yamato Meisho-zue)

apart and rebuilt at the new site.

In Nara, the Kondō (Main Hall) was and still is to this day the core of Yakushi-ji Temple. It comes into view immediately after entering the temple grounds through the Nandaimon (South Great Gate) and the Chūmon (Middle Gate). A cloister encircled the Main Hall linking the Middle Gate in the south with the Kōdō (Lecture Hall) in the north. Beyond the Lecture Hall stood the Shikidō (Refectory) and to the east and west of this the priestly quarters. The fact that Yakushi and not the historical Buddha Shaka is the temple's main object of worship may explain why the pagodas are not centrally located but are placed to the east and west of the Main Hall as if to flank it.

The Main Hall is noted for its outstanding statuary. The monumental statue of the Buddha of Healing, ruler of the eastern quarter of the Buddhist universe, is flanked by the bodhisattvas Nikkō (Sun) and Gakkō (Moon), the positioning of their inner arms creating an almost perfect harmony and symmetry. Adorning the Yakushi pedestal are two earthly genii and twelve peculiar creatures, half-naked cavemen peeping out from their primitive dwellings. They embody the Twelve Vows made by Yakushi to heal and assist all mankind, even uncivilized creatures such as these, who call upon him. These figures later evolved into the Jūni Jinshō (Twelve Divine Generals), the guardians of the zodiac and of all those who worship Buddhism, that one generally sees in Yakushi temples. The pedestal has other decorative designs, including the Chinese directional animals: the blue dragon of the east, the white tiger of the west, the phoenix of the south and the tortoise-serpent of the north. They symbolize the all-embracing powers of the Buddha. Yakushi-ji has another Yakushi triad in the Kōdō (Lecture Hall) which was part of an imperial palace before it was donated to the temple. This triad is of disputed origin and date and, though similar in many ways to the triad in the Main Hall, it is not artistically quite as perfect.

When Yakushi-ji was destroyed by fire in 974, nine provinces were ordered to assist in its rebuilding and the Shintō deity of war, Hachiman, was transferred from Usa in Kyūshū and installed, together with a statue of Empress Jingū, to protect the temple in the future. The two statues are still in Yakushi-ji's possession and are among the earliest specimens of Shintō art. When the temple burnt down yet again in 1448, funds for the reconstruction were solicited from as far away as Korea. The statues fortunately survived, no doubt saved from the flames at great human sacrifice.

The 34 meter high East Pagoda also miraculously survived the various conflagrations and is, therefore, one of the particularly priceless treasures from old Japan. There is no other pagoda in Japan with its apparently irregular shape, sometimes pointed to as an example of the innate Japanese taste for asymmetry and irregularity. Its appearance is deceptive: beneath each of the three main roofs is a smaller roof making it appear to have six stories when it has, in fact, only three. With the mingling of smaller and larger roofs, it seems as if two three-storied pagodas, one slightly larger than the other, were combined to create one single pagoda. The nine rings circling the spire denote the nine spheres of heaven. The spire culminates in a four-sided flame-shaped sphere ornamented with angels dancing and playing musical instruments as they descend from heaven. They are reminiscent of the music once played at the temple on certain festive occasions with instruments imported from the Continent and the Gigaku dances, also of foreign origin, which were performed to this musical accompaniment.

In the east of the Yakushi-ji compound is the Tōindō (East Temple Hall), a National Treasure remodeled in the Kamakura Period, which now serves as the temple's treasury. It contains a miniature model of the original Yakushi-ji — a device often used by temples as a replica to follow in rebuilding a temple after its destruction — and a painting on hemp of the goddess of learning, Kichijō-ten (here presented in the form of an aristocratic lady), who bestows good fortune on those who repent of their sins. The hall's main figure of

SHŌKANNON, Yakushi-ji Temple (Photo by courtesy of Kintetsu)

worship appears to be the bronze Shōkannon that was cast at the turn of the eighth century. The Shōkannon is the original Kannon and it is from this form that it transforms into the more than thirty shapes Kannon can assume on its missions to earth. The statue's eyes are filled with boundless mercy to alleviate the pains and sorrows worshippers might bring with them.

Of particular import to the study of the origin of the Japanese writing system is a stone in the Bussokudō (Hall of Buddha's Footprints) on which poems are inscribed using Chinese characters to represent Japanese sounds. Chinese characters usually convey an image or idea. This inscription is an early attempt in Japan to use the

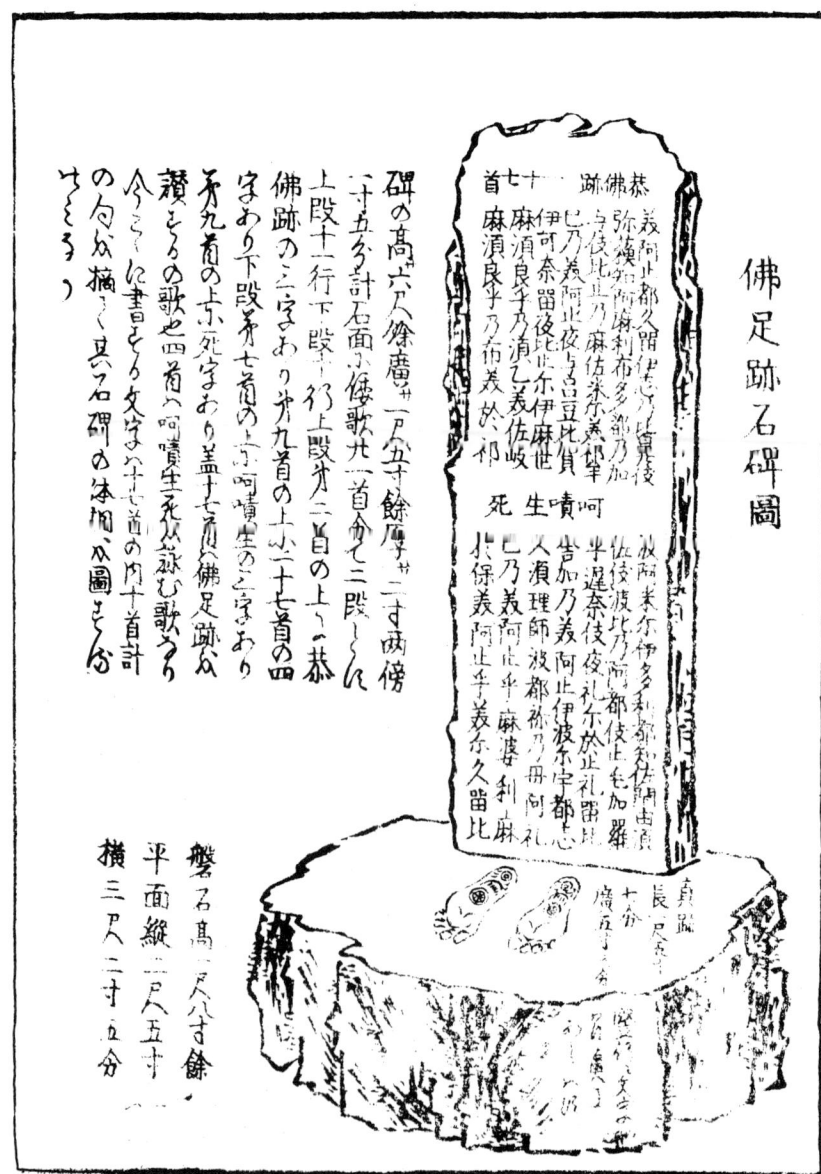

Buddha's Footprint Stone at Yakushi-ji Temple (*Yamato Meisho-zue*)

characters phonetically for their sounds instead and is one of the oldest traces of what later became the Japanese writing system. The 5 7 5 7 7 7 syllable poems praise the footprints of the Buddha which are carved onto another stone also kept in this hall. Footprints of the Buddha were carved into stone in India long before the meeting of Buddhist and Greek cultures led to the erecting of statues. Copies of the Buddha's footprints were originally taken from India to China and then eventually reached Japan, and represent an attempt, similar to stupas or pagodas to retain forever the traces of Buddha's life on earth. The Yakushi-ji footprints were made in 752 and later transferred to Nara from Fujiwara. To the north of the Eastern Pagoda stands a Bodai-ju (Bodhi) tree. While sitting under one of these trees in India the historical Buddha gained enlightenment. Like the footprints, this tree is a vestige of the earthly life of the Buddha.

With the exception of the East Pagoda, all buildings are later reconstructions. The Main Hall is a reconstruction from the year 1600; for centuries all that remained of the Western Pagoda were the foundation stones until it, too, was finally restored in 1981.

Tōshōdai-ji Temple: Lamenting the fact that no Japanese priest had received formal training in Buddhist discipline, and that the little discipline that existed was not rigorously enforced, Emperor Shōmu determined to invite a Chinese specialist in Buddhist discipline to Japan. He dispatched Priest Eiei of Daian-ji Temple and Priest Fushō of Kōfuku-ji Temple to China to seek out a master. The two priests embarked in 733 the boat of a Japanese ambassador and arrived safely despite the perils of the journey between the two countries. They searched in vain for about ten years until, at Ta-ming-ssu Temple in Yang-chou Province, they met Priest Chien-chen (Ganjin, in Japanese), a famous master of Buddhist monastic life. After hearing their request, Ganjin asked if any of his disciples would volunteer to go to Japan. None were willing to undertake the dangerous voyage. Declaring that Priest Hui-ssu, a precursor of the T'ien-T'ai (Tendai)

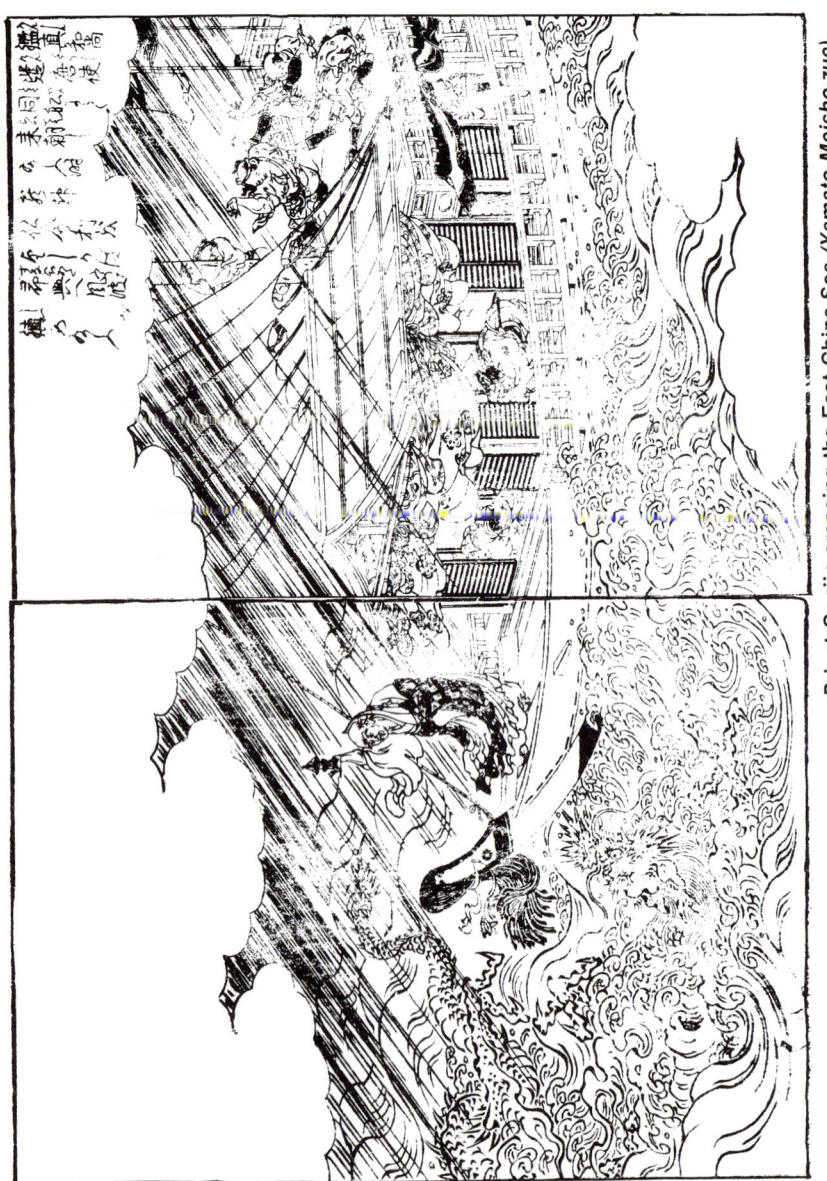

Priest Ganjin crossing the East China Sea (*Yamato Meisho-zue*)

School of Buddhism, had been reborn in Japan as Prince Shōtoku in order to promote Buddhism there, Ganjin boldly decided to personally accept the invitation to go to Japan despite his age of fifty-five. He appointed twenty-one disciples and, in addition, painters, sculptors and embroiderers to accompany him, an entourage of 185 persons in all.

It was another ten years before Ganjin was able to reach Japan. Four attempts to cross the sea were frustrated. First, two of his disciples were accused of being pirates; the second attempt ended in shipwreck and the crew were taken back to China; the third time, adverse winds blew the ship in the opposite direction to Hainan Island; and on the fourth attempt officials refused to allow a priest as eminent as Ganjin to leave the country. His party shrank with each failure. After the fourth attempt, Ganjin, suffering from an eye disease, went blind. Undaunted, he was finally able to board the ship of a Japanese vice-ambassador in 750 and safely arrived in Nara in 754 travelling by way of Okinawa. He was first housed at Tōdai-ji Temple and endowed with 250 acres of rice fields for his and his attendants' sustenance.

Certain that his life was drawing to a close, Ganjin wasted no time in instructing a body of Japanese disciples in his school of discipline, called Ritsu. In 762, he received permission to ordain priests. An ordination platform was built in the main courtyard of Tōdai-ji and there he formally ordained a group of well-trained monks in front of the emperor and 450 officials and priests. In addition to his function as a teacher of Buddhist discipline, Ganjin acted as advisor on Buddhist matters to Emperor Shōmu, the empress and crown princess. He lectured and commented upon the sutras he had brought with him from China. When given permission to return to his homeland he refused. Indebted to Ganjin for his services, the Emperor presented him with land, the means to build a retreat in Western Nara, and a residence once used by a prince. This became Tōshōdai-ji Temple in 759 and is still one of the most beautiful temples in the Nara area.

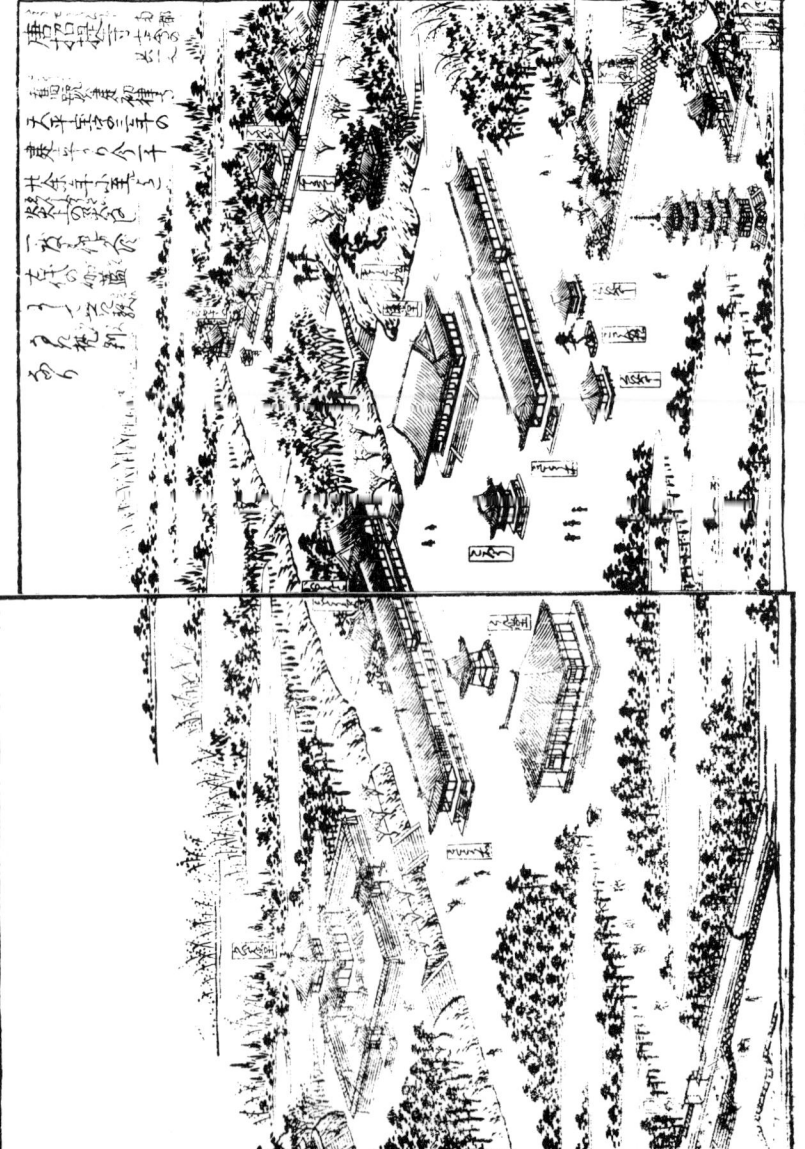

Tōshōdai-ji Temple (Yamato Meisho-zue)

Ganjin's Ritsu Sect, which emphasized discipline over doctrine, was firmly established in Japan with the building of this temple.

The Nandaimon (South Great Gate), a Chūmon (Middle Gate) that no longer exists, a Kondō (Main Hall) and a Kōdō (Lecture Hall) formed a single line and all faced toward the south. A cloister linked the Middle Gate in the south with the Main Hall in the north creating a large, open courtyard. Between the Main and Lecture Halls stood, to the east and west respectively, a Drum Tower and a Belfry, necessary devices to impose strict discipline over and to regulate the daily lives of the monks. The Lecture Hall had been part of the Chōdōin (Morning Assembly Hall) at the Nara imperial palace, then attached to a princely residence built in the same area as Tōshōdai-ji before becoming a part of the temple. The now no longer extant Refectory, located behind the Lecture Hall, was a gift from a powerful Fujiwara. Emperor Heizei (r. 806-809) donated a five-storied pagoda (Tōtō) in 810 which was built in the southeastern corner of the temple, but it has not survived either. To the east and west of the Lecture Hall were the priestly quarters. One of these buildings was also a Fujiwara gift. East of the Eastern Priestly Quarters (Tōjitsu) were the three, eighth century log cabins composing the Kyōzō (Sutra Repositories) that dates back to the eighth century.

Today, a lovely tree-lined avenue leads up to the Main Hall. The imposing roof finials were crafted in the Nara Period. The colonnade of eight pillars at the entrance of the hall has often been attributed to the influence of Greek temples. Inside, the paintings of the panels and pillars depict the Three Thousand Buddha Worlds, all of which issue from Dainichi according to the *Bonmō-kyō* Sutra. The dry lacquer statue of the Buddha Dainichi, apparently crafted by one of Ganjin's Chinese disciples, is three meters tall and stands on a two-meter high lotus pedestal. There are Buddhas on each of the flower's petals. The halo, five meters in height, is formed by clusters of Buddhas totalling one thousand in all that are said to have emanated from the primordial Dainichi. The Buddha's grave facial expression reflects the severity of

SENJU (THOUSAND-HANDED) KANNON, Tōshōdai-ji Temple

Ganjin's Ritu discipline.

It is flanked by a standing Yakushi and a Senju (Thousand-armed) Kannon. Repairs on the Yakushi statue in 1972 revealed that it was carved in about 796. The Thousand-armed Kannon, from the Nara Period, measures five and a half meters and is the oldest and largest of its kind in Japan. Forty-eight of its one thousand hands have been lost but it retains, nevertheless, more of its hands than any other statue of its kind.

Each of the four corners of the altar is typically guarded by one of the Shitennō (Four Heavenly Kings) — Bon-ten, Taishaku-ten, Jigoku-ten and Zōchō-ten. These statues preserve a Nara Period atmosphere and are all National Treasures. The 1.8 meter high wooden statues of Bon-ten and Taishaku-ten originally had lacquered surfaces. Comic figures are painted on their pedestals.

Worshippers were not permitted inside the Main Hall as it was Buddha's sacred abode, and no space was provided for a large number of worshippers. Instead they prayed from just outside the hall regardless of the weather. Two lanterns shed light not on the statues but on the worshippers, for they had to be seen by the Buddha and not vice-versa. Only one lantern remains today.

The Lecture Hall, constructed during Nara times, contains as its central object of worship a Miroku, the Buddha of the Future who, when the world comes to an end 5,600,000,000 years after the death of the historical Buddha, will descend to earth in the stead of Shaka to save all those remaining to be saved. The statue dates from the Kamakura Period and is attended by a Jigoku-ten and Zōchō-ten.

The Ordination Platform (Kaidan) in the west of the compound was probably transferred from Tōdai-ji where Ganjin ordained the first priests. The Kaisandō (Founder's Hall), also known as Hongandō, houses the famous statue of Ganjin carved in 763 after one of his disciples had a dream foretelling the priest's imminent death. The disciples decided a statue of their master should be carved quickly before he died. The result was this statue which is the oldest portrait in Japan and a superior work of art. Though blind, Ganjin appears to be watching intensely all that is going on around him. In a sense, this statue is the soul of Tōshōdai-ji. Bashō (1644-1694), one of Japan's most outstanding poets, composed the following poem about Ganjin's statue:

Now, that the young leaves are out,
If only I could wipe off
The dew drops from underneath your eyes.

TEMPLES OUTSIDE THE NARA CAPITAL

Taima-dera Temple: In the Jinshin War, a succession struggle in 672,
Temmu allied himself with the powerful Taima Clan in his bid for the
emperorship. The Taima, based at the foot of Mt. Nijō, were one of
the clans to embrace Buddhism. Their family temple was located on
roughly the same site today occupied by Taima-dera Temple. After
Temmu's successful conclusion of the Jinshin War and his installation
as emperor, the temple was enlarged in 681 and a statue of En no
Gyōja (d. ca 715), the legendary founder of the Yamabushi (Mountain
Anchorites), was installed inside a statue of Miroku worshipped by the
Taima in the Kondō (Main Hall). The Yamabushi, priests who
performed austerities in the mountains in order to be instilled with
magical powers, played a vital role in the synthesis of Buddhism and
Shintō. En no Gyōja apparently came from the Taima area and
allegedly gained his magical powers in the mountains of Katsuragi and
Nijō.

    According to another version of the temple's origins, it was
Prince Maroko, the founder of the Taima Clan and an adherent of
Prince Shōtoku, who founded Taima-dera in 612. He apparently
installed the En no Gyōja statue after receiving instructions to do so in
a dream. The first version appears however to be a more plausible
explanation of the temple's founding. Such conflicting versions about
the origins of temples often obscure the historical facts but prove that
such traditions were transmitted by people for whom legend was often
more important than history.

    After its expansion, the temple's main structures came to include a

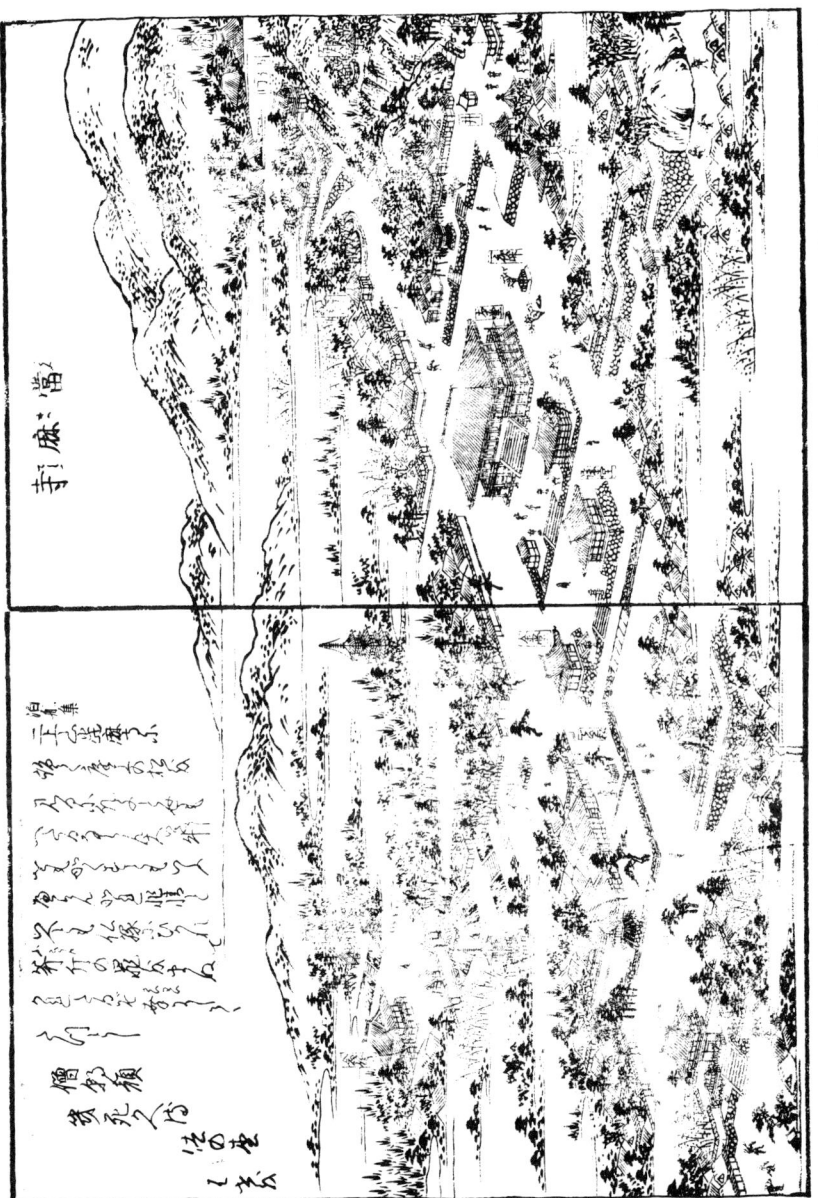

Taima-dera Temple (*Yamato Meisho-zue*)

132

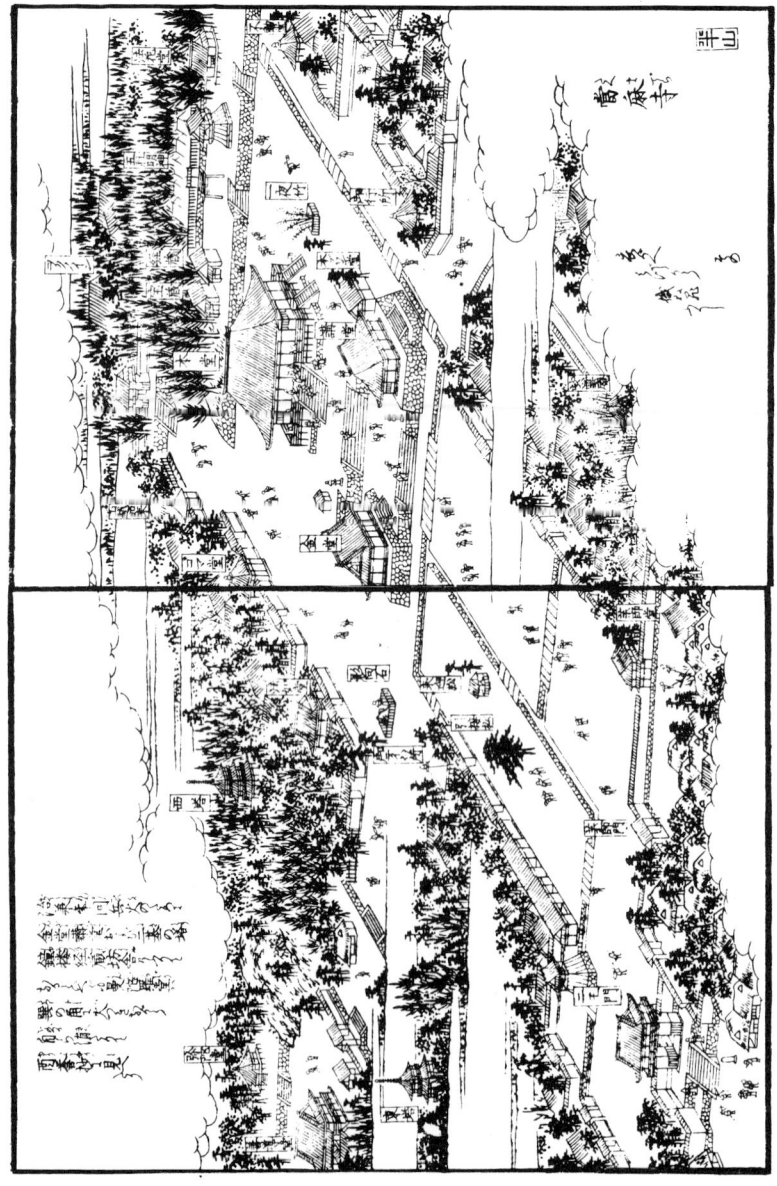

Taima-dera Temple (Saikoku Meisho-zue)

Nandaimon (South Great Gate), a Kondō (Main Hall) and a Kōdō (Lecture Hall). These were lined up along a north to south axis and two three-storied pagodas built in the east and the west of the compound. They still stand today, having withstood the vicissitudes of history and nature. The Belfry, located near the Higashimon (East Gate), today is among the oldest extant belfries in Japan. The dried clay statue of Miroku in the Main Hall and the Shitennō (Four Heavenly Kings) which surround it are Nara Period sculptures. Perhaps because the beards of the Kings struck the Japanese as rather exotic, the statues were thought to have originated in Paekché. Zōchō-ten (one of the Heavenly Kings) in particular looks Central Asian.

A miracle in 763 was to alter the course of Taima-dera's future. In that year, legend has it, in answer to a prayer a certain Princess Chūjō in retirement at the temple weaved a mandala with lotus fiber in the course of a single night. The mandala pictorially represented the Western Paradise of the Buddha of Mercy, Amida. Princess Chūjō, whose priestly name was Honnyo, is still remembered on May 14 every year when her entry into paradise is symbolically re-enacted by 25 priests. The priests represent the twenty-five bodhisattva attendants of Amida who cross over a bridge symbolically spanning the abyss separating heaven and earth to collect souls for paradise. The priests come for the souls of Princess Chūjō by walking along an avenue in the temple ground which runs from east to west and which, in an imaginary continuation, links up with the pass that lies between the male (515m) and the female (474m) peaks of Mt. Nijō in the West. The Raigō* painting, *Yamagoshi Amida-zu*, in Taima-dera's possession shows Amida waiting beyond the pass of Mt. Nijō to receive souls into his paradisiacal realm. This painting is yet another indication of the Japanese belief that Mt. Nijō is the abode of the dead.

---

* Raigō are paintings depicting Amida's descent to earth to guide the souls of the dead to his Western paradise.

134

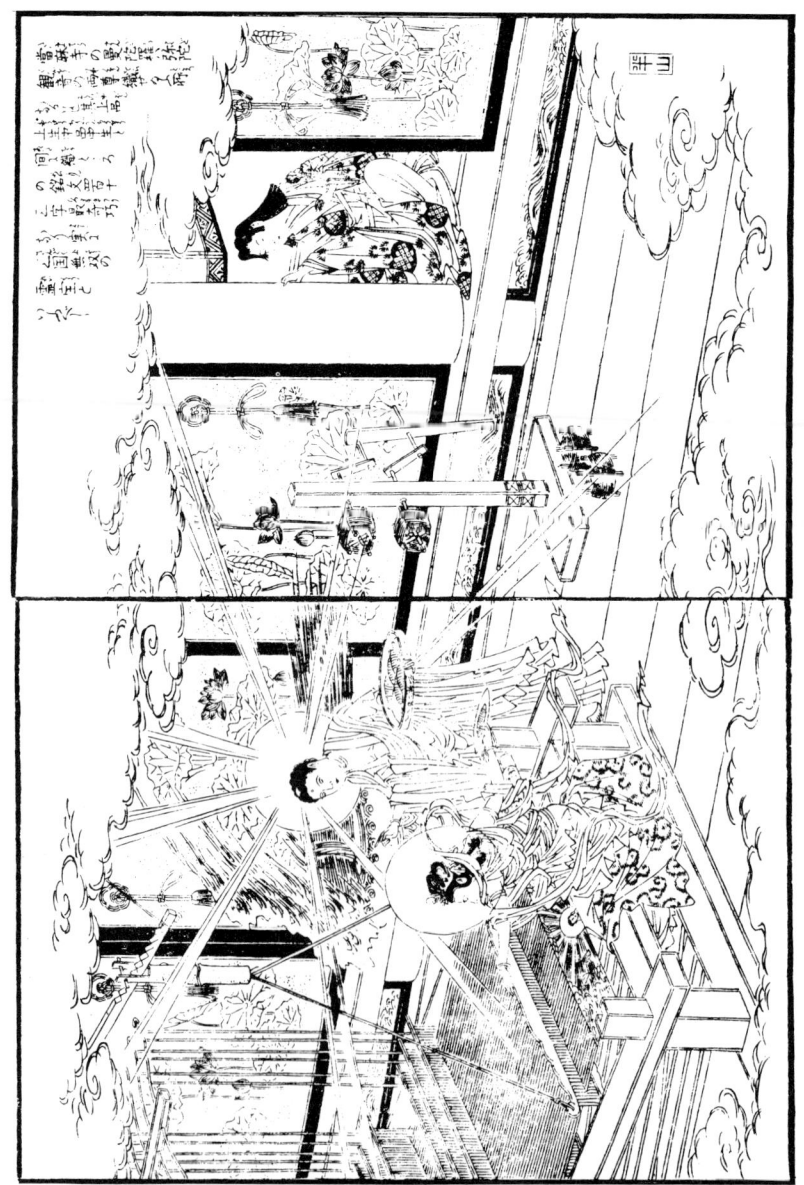

Princess Chūjō Weaving the Taima Mandala *(Saikoku Meisho-zue)*

Princess Chūjō's mandala, known as *Taima Mandala,* became the object of nationwide veneration after the year 1052, the year in which Mappō, the End of Buddhist Law Period, was supposed to begin. Mappō had been prophesized as an age of chaos, decadence and crime that would begin two thousand years after the death of Buddha. Mappō would last 10,000 years and would lead to the eventual destruction of the world. Believing that man's only hope was reliance on the Buddha Amida, the popularity of sects such as the Jōdo (Pure Land) and Jōdo Shin (True Pure Land) which emphasized faith in Amida alone soared. Pilgrimages to Taima-dera to worship before the *Taima Mandala* reached unprecedented levels and donations flooded in even from the imperial family. Copies of the mandala were made for distribution to other temples. The Kondō was replaced as Main Hall by the Mandaladō (Mandala Hall) built behind the Main and Lecture Halls in the west of the complex. It was reached by passing through the Higashimon (East Gate) which faced towards the west. The new focus of the temple altered its north-south orientation to east-west so that it faced Amida's Western Paradise thought to lie beyond the pass between Mt. Nijō's twin peaks.

The Mandala Hall, designated as a National Treasure in 1962, has been repaired about ten times. The *Taima Mandala* has been restored several times. When it became too faded a new one was woven, not in one night but between the years 1487 and 1489, and the original preserved in the temple's Treasury.

Hase-dera Temple:

> The mountains of Hatsuse [Hase]
> > The secluded —
> They stand out
> Excellent mountains!
> They run out
> Excellent mountains!
> The mountains of Hatsuse,

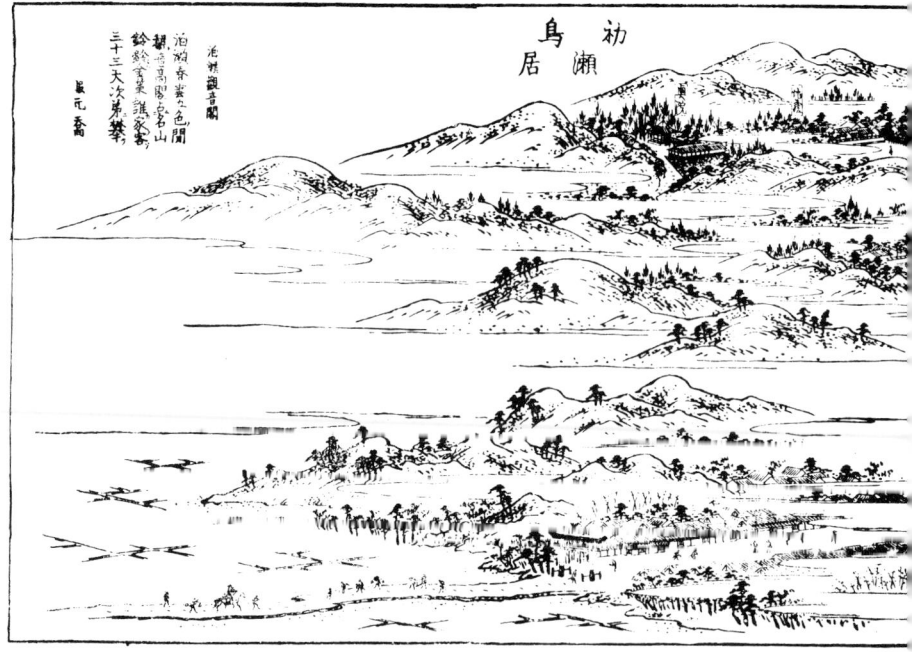

Hase-dera Temple *(Yamato Meisho-zue)*

The secluded —
Are full of various beauties!
Are full of various beauties!

(Nihon Shoki)

A simple statement of when, where and by whom Hase-dera Temple was built is not sufficient for an understanding of this temple. It is necessary to return to pre-Nara times and the cult of the dead observed in the Hase area. Hase was given the epithet of *komoriku*, or "secluded place" in ancient Japanese poetry because it was revered as the abode of the dead.

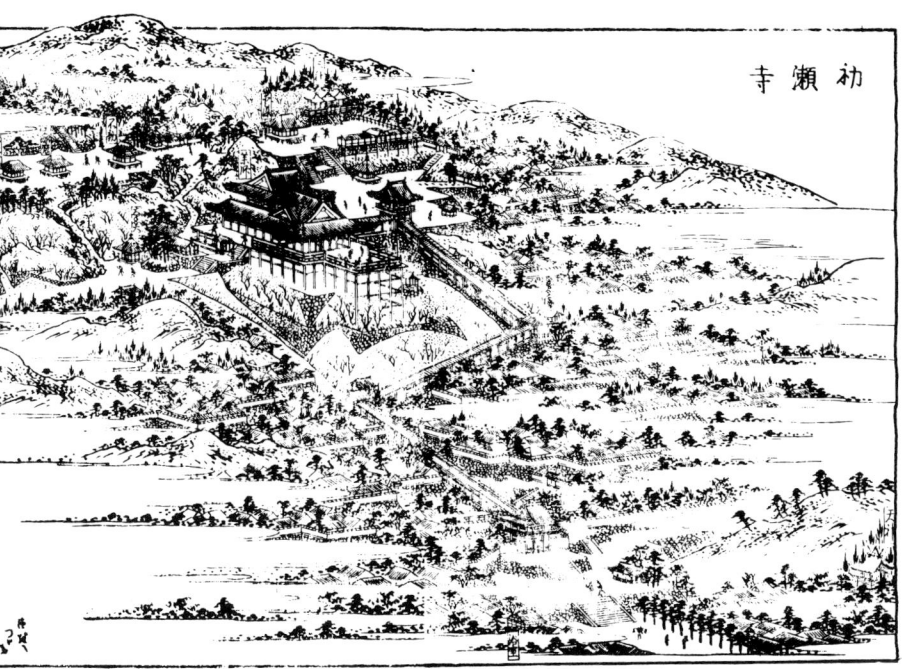

初瀬寺

At the cremation of the Maiden of Hijikata on the hills Hatsuse.

The cloud drifting over the brows
    Of the hills of secluded Hatsuse —
Can it, alas, be she?

                            (Manyōshū)

The cult may have been one of the reasons why the priest Dōmyō (dates unknown) chose Hase as the site for the three-storied pagoda, Senbetsu Tahō-tō, dedicated to the *Lotus Sutra* as a votive prayer for the afterlife of Emperor Temmu.

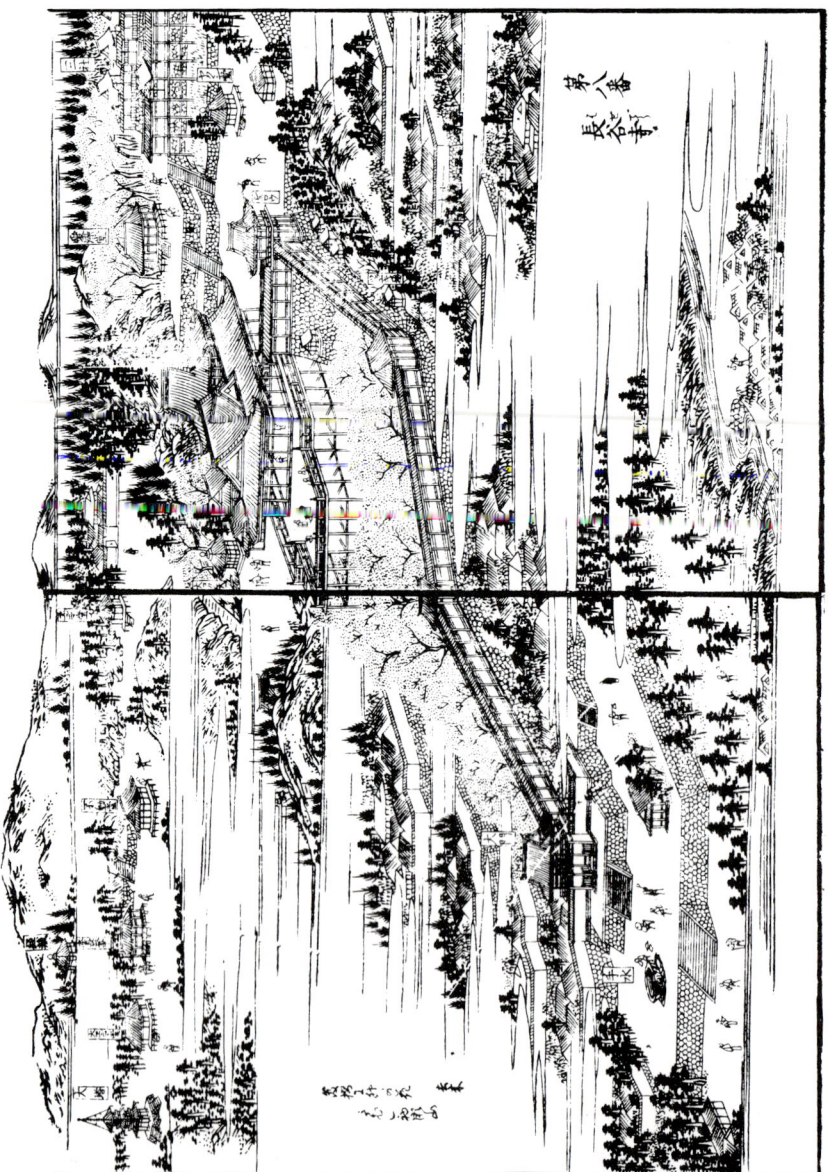

Hase-dera Temple (*Saikoku Meisho-zue*)

Dōmyō also saw in the Hase mountains a substitute for the Sacred Vulture Peak in India where the historical Buddha Shaka expounded the *Lotus Sutra*. For the same reason, the main object of worship at the temple that flourished around the pagoda was a copperplate with a frontal relief portraying the Buddha preaching the *Lotus Sutra*. He is surrounded not only by his disciples but also by Buddhas and bodhisattvas who have flocked together from the entire Buddhist universe to listen to him. In the center of the relief a hexagonal three-storied pagoda is depicted. On the first floor of the pagoda is the historical Buddha and a Tahō (Many Treasure) Buddha who is said to appear on earth wherever and whenever necessary in order to explain the *Lotus Sutra*. On the bottom of the relief is an inscription recording the founding of Hase-dera by Dōmyō in 686. The origin of the plate, cast in 686, 698 or 710 depending on the theory, remains obscure, although similar pictorial representations can be found in China. The copperplate is still counted among the priceless treasures of the Hase-dera.

Dōmyō's three-storied pagoda burnt down in 1876 but in 1952, not far from where it once stood, a five-storied pagoda was built. This portion of Hase-dera Temple that was founded in 686 came to be called Motohase-dera (Original Hase) Temple when it received an addition centered upon a Kannon. It was Emperor Shōmu who ordered Priest Tokudō, a disciple of Dōmyō, to install a Kannon statue in the Hase-dera. Priest Tokudō (b. 656) was told in a dream where to find a sacred tree from which to carve the statue. Tradition has it that the two sculptors he commissioned were able to finish the statue in a mere three days in 729 thanks to the intensive prayers of Tokudō. The result was an imposing Jūichimen (Eleven-headed) Kannon, carved according to a description in the *Jūichimen Kannon-gyō* Sutra. It was housed in a hall which became part of the Nochibase-dera or Later Hase Temple. The Kannon statue was duly inaugurated in 733 with Priest Gyōgi and the Indian priest Bodaisenna (Bodhisena) officiating. In keeping with the merging of Buddhism and Shintō the

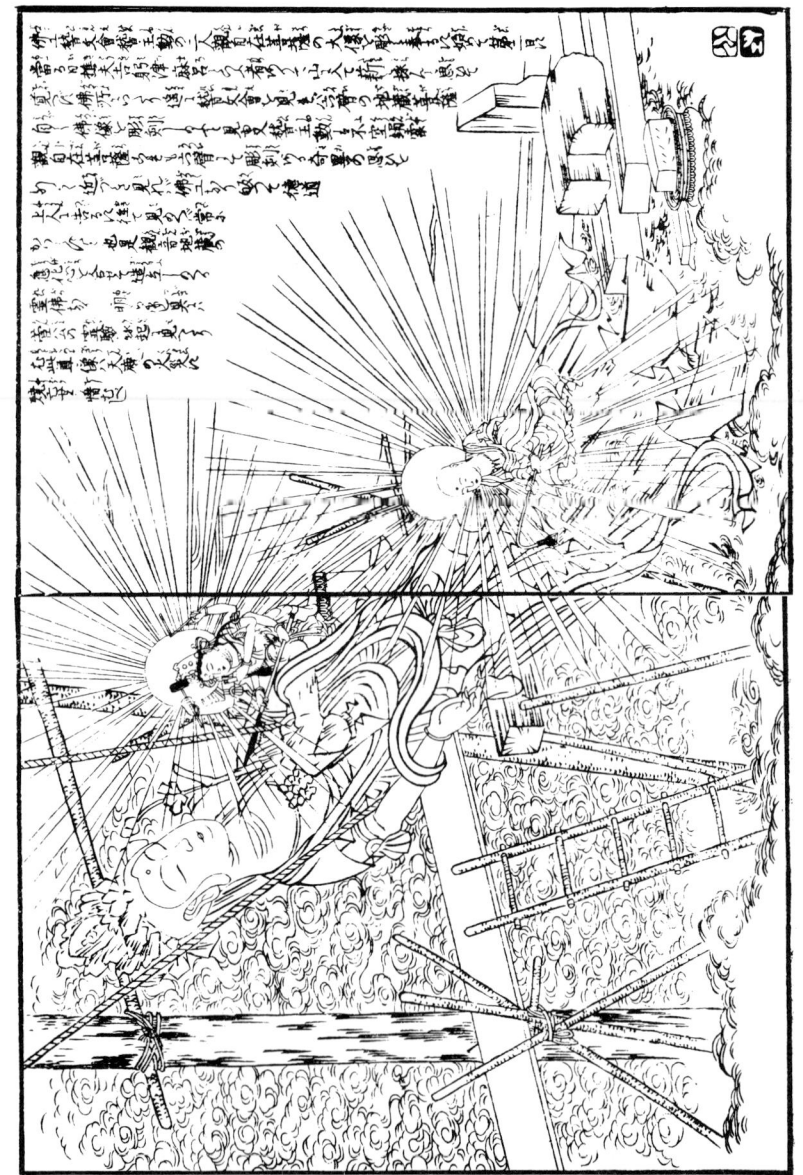

Miraculous carving of the Jūichimen (Eleven-headed) Kanron at Hase-dera Temple (*Saikoku Meisho-zue*)

JŪICHIMEN (ELEVEN-HEADED) KANNON, Hase-dera Temple

Sun Goddess Amaterasu, the deity from whom the present imperial line sprang, was considered the Shintō manifestation of the Hase Kannon. The Kannon statue was damaged by fire several times. The present statue was sculpted by a Kyoto sculptor in 1538. The emotional expressions on the ten faces crowning its head are varied and include gentleness, anger, sadness, wisdom and joy. The staff held in its right hand resembles the staffs held by statues of the bodhisattva

Jizō and evokes an image of the Kannon in his indefatigable quest to save souls travelling through Rokudō (Six Paths) — the six realms between and including hell and heaven.

The Hondō (Main Hall) is built on a system of pillars in an imaginary representation of the Southern Paradise of Kannon. The stairway leading up to the hall, built in 1039 with the funds provided by an official of the Kasuga Shrine, is one hundred and eight *kan* (spaces between pillars) long denoting the one hundred and eight sins a man is likely to commit in the course of a year. Pilgrims exonerate themselves of their sins by climbing this stairway.

In the Heian Period, Hase-dera became a center of pilgrimage for both men and women. Women were not allowed to worship at many temples (for example, the Shingon* Temple on Mt. Koya) for they were thought to be unable to attain salvation. Hase-dera welcomed women because of its association with the *Lotus Sutra* in which a woman attains enlightenment. In addition, although the Kannon was ascribed male characteristics in China, it was a female bodhisattva in Japan. Thus Hase-dera frequently appears in the literary works written by court ladies during the Heian Period.

The Hase Kannon gained greater fame as a result of legends extolling its miraculous powers. These, it seems, reached as far as China; after praying to this Kannon an ugly concubine (legend tells us she had the face of a horse) of a T'ang Dynasty emperor was transformed into a beauty. The grateful lady is supposed to have been the donor of the peonies which have bloomed for centuries in the temple grounds and continue to be the pride of Hase-dera. They immerse the temple in their lively hues when they bloom in late April or early May.

---

* Shingon (Mantra) Buddhism was an esoteric sect of Buddhism introduced in the early ninth century by Kūkai (posthumously Kōbō Daishi, 774-835).

Murō-ji Temple: Like Hase-dera, Murō-ji (Cave) Temple was established in an area reverenced as sacred from ancient times. The waterfalls especially were venerated as the abode of the dragon deity who controlled rain and was therefore closely linked with fertility. Dragons lived in ponds, lakes, waterfall pools and rain clouds according to popular belief. The dragon deity at Murō-ji apparently inhabited the Sarusawa Pond in Nara, but when, having been abandoned by the emperor, an imperial concubine polluted the dragon's abode by drowning herself in the pond, the deity escaped to the waterfalls in the vicinity of Murō-ji. En no Gyōja, a kind of Taoist miracle maker already mentioned, was able to locate the dragon by magical means and had Ryūketsu (Dragon Cave) Shrine built.

Murō-ji's history began around 771 or 778 when Emperor Kammu (r. 781-806), still crown prince at the time, fell seriously ill. Kōfuku-ji priests were dispatched to Murō to recite sutras at Ryūketsu Shrine. When the crown prince recovered, Murō-ji was built nearby. Priest Kenkai of Kōfuku-ji, a known geomancer who had been ordained by Ganjin, was put in charge of its construction. The real purpose behind Murō-ji Temple was to encourage further synthesis of Buddhism and Shintō by enshrining the dragon deity, who had come to be regarded as a divinity of both religions.

Both Hase-dera and Murō-ji are mountain temples and consequently deviated considerably from the symmetrical organization of lowland temples. Murō-ji's Niōmon (Niō Gate), Kondō (Main Hall), Mirokudō (Miroku Hall), Hondō (Main Hall) and a five-storied pagoda which make up the complex are arranged haphazardly on a slope. Further uphill is the Oku no In (Back Temple). Many mountain temples had Oku no In reached by a walk deep into the hills along a path that was lined with stone Buddhas. Due to the influence of Shingon Buddhism, Murō-ji came to be considered as part of a natural mandala, a miniature of the Buddhist universe approached by a bridge over the Murō River that linked the secular world with the sacred world of the temples. Shingon stressed the use of mandalas as objects

JŪICHIMEN (ELEVEN-HEADED) KANNON, Murō-ji Temple

of meditation with which worshippers tried to grasp the essence of the universe. In this case the mountains of Murō were seen as the lotus seats of Buddhas and bodhisattvas in the mandalas.

The pagoda here is particularly noteworthy. First built in 780, it measures about sixteen meters and its roofs are thatched with cypress bark. The Kondō contains a Shaka flanked by Yakushi and a Jizō to its left and a Jūichimen (Eleven-headed) Kannon and a Monju to its right. The Shaka, Yakushi and Kannon are National Treasures. In front of

SHAKA, Miroku Hall, Murō-ji Temple

these stand the Twelve Divine Generals, attendants of Yakushi. A statue of Miroku attended by a seated Shaka, also a National Treasure, can be found in the Miroku Hall. The Kanchōdō contains a statue of a seated Nyoirin Kannon, a bodhisattva who fulfills all wishes and delivers people from suffering, which is the main object of worship at Murō-ji Temple. None of these treasures appear to date from the Nara Period but are probably later works of art.

Not far from Murō-ji is a large Miroku that was hewn into a cliff by Chinese craftsmen between 1207 and 1208. It is the largest of its kind in Japan.

Because of its connection with the dragon deity, in times of drought prayers for rain were often offered here by imperial messengers by reading sutras. The first one recorded took place in 781. The temple also possesses a *Taishaku Mandala* that portrays Indra, originally a Hindu deity, in his role as a rain-maker, perhaps because Kūkai, Shingon's founder, had a reputation as a skilled rain-maker.

Like Hase-dera, Murō-ji too allowed women into its precincts to worship. Since the head temples of the Shingon Sect on Mt. Kōya refused to accept women, Murō-ji Temple came to be known as the "Mt. Kōya of Women."

Shinyakushi-ji (New Yakushi-ji) Temple: To reach Shinyakushi-ji Temple one treads upon the ancient Yagyū Road, that once linked Nara and the village of Yagyū before continuing on to Mt. Kasagi. The road passes old mud walls, one of which was once a part of the former residence of the modern Japanese writer Shiga Naoya, and on through a breath-taking rural area of Nara which preserves a solemn atmosphere of antiquity. Formerly the Yagyū Road was used by Kōfuku-ji monks on their way to present prayers to the Stone Buddhas in the mountains of Kasuga. In Nara times this was a famous locale for viewing the moon, a popular pastime of the aristocracy. Here is a poem composed in the area:

> Is it because Mt. Takamado
> Is so tall
> That the moon
> Is so late to shine?
>
> *(Manyōshū)*

Empress Kōmyō commissioned the construction of the Shinyakushi-ji in 747 as a prayer for the recovery of Emperor Shōmu. The temple was combined with an earlier Yakushi temple called Kōzan Yakushi-ji which had been erected in the Kasuga mountains also by Empress Kōmyō. Forty-nine priests were ordered to serve the new temple and to worship the Yakushi installed within.

YAKUSHI, Shinyakushi-ji Temple

The only remaining major structure of what was once a much larger temple complex is the Hondō (Main Hall), a National Treasure. In the opinion of some specialists, the Hondō was the original Shikidō (Refectory) and not, as others claim, the original Kondō (Main Hall). The present East and South Gates are all Kamakura Period reconstructions. The South Gate originally linked up with Go-jō (Fifth Street) in Nara. The Yakushi statue in the Main Hall is also a National Treasure and is probably a later statue dating from the early Heian Period. The original was in all likelihood lost in a fire in 780 caused by lightning. On the halo are depicted the Seven Buddhas who preside over the seven sub-areas of the Eastern Paradise of Yakushi.

YAKUSHI AND TWELVE DIVINE GENERALS, Shinyakushi-ji Temple

Of particular interest in the Main Hall are the Twelve Generals
(Jūni Jinshō) who incorporate the Twelve Vows of Yakushi. They
protect Yakushi's Jōruri, or Eastern Paradise, from evil. Haira, left
arm akimbo, holds a spear in his right hand; Basara holds a horsehair
flapper with both hands; Indara, right arm akimbo, stretches his left
arm; while Antera, left hand on his waist, holds a spear in his other
hand. Shindara has a jewelled stick in his left hand and a jewel in his
right; and Santera holds a sword in his left hand and splays the fingers
of his right hand at his waist. Shotora's hair stands up on end like
spikes, his mouth is wide open to emit a savage yell, and he threatens
with the sword he clutches in his right hand. Makora grasps an ax in
his right hand and his left rests on his waist; Bikara holds up a pounder

BASARA, ONE OF THE TWELVE DIVINE GENERALS, Shinyakushi-ji Temple

with his right arm; Kubira is about to fix an arrow in his bow; Anira holds an arrow in both hands; and Mekira grasps a sword in his right hand.* Each general wears Chinese military dress, some of which, Shotora's, for example, are beautifully decorated. The twelve statues probably date from the Nara Period and, with the exception of Kubira, are National Treasures.

---

* In naming these statues, I followed the Japanese Commission on National Treasures. Shinyakushi-ji tradition attributes different names to some of them.

On April 8 each year in a Shuni-e festival, twelve huge torches are burnt while twelve priests, representing the Twelve Generals, recite from a sutra. This festival is similar to the Shuni-e (Mizutori) at Tōdai-ji Temple. This can be interpreted as a festival of renewal in which the old is burnt to give way to the new.

Not far to the south of Shinyakushi-ji Temple, at the foot of Mt. Takamado, is another Nara Period temple, the Byakugō-ji. The grounds of this temple, that grew out of a princely retreat in 715, command a panoramic view of the Yamato Plain. The temple declined in the Heian Period but was later revived by Priest Eison of Saidai-ji Temple. In the Hondō (Main Hall) is a Nara Period statue of Amida sitting. Many of the other statues date from later periods.

Temples and stone Buddhas in the Kasagi mountains: In days gone by, the priests of Tōdai-ji and Kōfuku-ji used to undergo austerities in the gentle, green hills between Nara and the village of Yagyū. This probably accounts for the many stone Buddhas one can find, sometimes deeply embedded, in these hills that were once the sacred hinterland of Nara. The largest is a Miroku hewn into a rock on Mt. Kasagi sometime during the years when Nara was capital. A number of stone Buddhas are also to be found in caves in the area. The most famous, including a Dainichi and a Miroku Buddha, are located at Jigoku-dani (Hell Valley), and others at Ishikiri-tōge Pass.

There are also a number of Nara Period temples in these hills. Gansen-ji was founded in 729 at the wish of Emperor Shōmu and consisted initially of thirty-nine halls. It burnt down in 1221. Among the treasures of this temple are a thirteen-storied stone pagoda from the Kamakura Period, a three-storied pagoda from the 14th century and a Heian Period statue of Amida, all of which have been designated as Important Cultural Properties.

Walking from Gansen-ji to Jōruri-dera Temple one sees again many stone Buddhas, Jizōs, Amidas and Fudōs. The Jōruri-dera (also Kutai-ji) is said to have been founded by the charismatic priest Gyōgi (who was given the title of bodhisattva) in 743. It had as its main figure a Yakushi and for this reason was named Jōruri, indicating the Jōruri Eastern Paradise over which Yakushi rules. Jōruri-dera is known particularly for its Kuhon Amida, nine Heian Period Amida statues installed in the Hondō (Main Hall). The nine statues refer to the nine categories of human souls who enter Amida's paradise by enduring nine forms of hardship. They also indicate Amida's will to save even the most wicked of mankind. The statues and the Hall are all National Treasures. Worshippers were not allowed inside this Main Hall but had to present their petitions from the far side of a pond. The pond symbolically separated the secular from the world of Amida, a world reachable in reality only after death.

The exact circumstances of the founding of Enshō-ji, another temple in the Kasagi hills, remain shrouded in mystery. All that is known is that the temple was built at the foot of Mt. Ninniku to symbolize one of the Six Stages (Rokuharamitsu) of the bodhisattva's long journey to the World of the Buddhas, and was founded in 756 by Korō, who is thought to have been one of the Chinese priests who accompanied Ganjin to Japan. Enshō-ji was expanded in 1153 by a Kyoto priest. The present Hondō (Main Hall) is a Muromachi Period (1334-1568) reconstruction. It houses a Heian Period statue of Amida sitting surrounded by statues of the Shitennō, the Four Heavenly Kings, carved in the Kamakura Period. It also contains a statue of Dainichi carved by the renowned Unkei in 1196. The pond in front of Enshō-ji dates back to the temple's inception when an Eleven-headed Kannon (Jūichimen) was the temple's central figure of worship. The pond symbolizes the ocean in front of the Potalaka (Fudaraku, in Japanese), the Southern Paradise of Kannon.

In its grounds are two Shintō shrines, Kasugadō and Hakusandō, both of which are National Treasures. They were built in 1228 when Buddhism had already firmly merged with Shintō and it was a general policy to build Shintō shrines in temple grounds and temples near shrines. By this time Buddhas had come to be regarded as Shintō

忍辱山圓成寺之景

Ninniku-sen Enshō-ji Temple (Yamato Meisho-zue)

deities and vice versa.

Hannya-ji Temple: The prevalence of various stories concerning Hannya-ji Temple's early days obscure the actual facts of its origin. According to one tradition, Hannya-ji was founded in 629 by the Korean priest Ekan, founder of the Sanron sect, four years after he came to Japan. Another claims that Emperor Shōmu founded the temple to the northeast of the capital in order to protect the imperial palace from evil, which was thought always to enter an area from the northeast; while yet another account suggests that Hannya-ji was constructed after Shōmu's death as a prayer for his afterlife, and names Priest Gyōgi as its first head priest. These are only three of the variations that succeed in clouding all but the fact that it was indeed founded in the Nara Period. This is evident from a reference to the temple in a 742 entry in a document preserved at Shōsō-in Repository at Tōdai-ji.

Hannya-ji was built on top of the Nara Slope. Used as a burial ground, it was also known by the Buddhist name of Hannya-zaka (Hannya Slope). The word Hannya refers to the true wisdom from which enlightenment and salvation spring. The temple is closely associated with Monju, the bodhisattva of Supreme Wisdom, who, according to the *Kegon-kyō* Sutra, resides in the east or northeast of the Buddhist universe. He is the Buddha Shaka's left-hand attendant and is respected as the personification of Buddha's wisdom.

Like most Nara temples, Hannya-ji was razed to the ground by Taira no Shigehira in 1180. When Shigehira was later captured and put to death, his head was reportedly displayed in the temple. Hannya-ji was rebuilt in 1240 with a thirteen-storied stone pagoda at its center. A statue of Monju was installed in the Hondō (Main Hall) about 20 years later. In the *Monju-gyō* Sutra, Monju promises that any one simply hearing his name or seeing a statue representing him will be saved from committing evil and whoever calls out his name will be reborn in paradise. In the *Monju-hannya-gyō* Sutra, the doctrine that all

154

Hannya-ji Temple (*Yamato Meisho-zue*)

things, including life itself, are ultimately meaningless is set forth.

The treasures of Hannya-ji Temple include the Rōmon (Tower Gate), a National Treasure built in the Kamakura Period during the temple's reconstruction. The thirteen-storied stone pagoda still stands, and is an Important Cultural Property. The statue of Monju seated on a lotus flower that balances on the back of a lion — an animal tamed by Monju — is in the Main Hall surrounded by the Four Heavenly Kings. This is not the original statue, however. The Main Hall together with the original Monju burnt down in 1490. The present Monju was taken from the Kyōzō (Sutra Repository) and installed in the new hall.

Further down the slope from Hannya-ji in the direction of Nara is an historic building that was used as a leprosarium until the end of the 19th century. Built by Priest Ninshō (1217-1303), who engaged in social work in that area, it was probably one of Japan's first leprosariums. It was not always located at its present site but was relocated here between 1661 and 1673 to take advantage of the view of Tōdai-ji's Great Buddha Hall and Kōfuku-ji's five-storied pagoda.

NARA SHRINES

Kasuga Taisha Shrine: Old stone lanterns line the avenue leading to Kasuga Taisha Shrine and sacred deer roam its grounds at will. Located within a forest of tall, venerable trees, the shrine occupies one of the most picturesque sites in Nara. Like the numerous Nara temples, this shrine is intimately linked with the period when Nara was capital, its flourishing and its decline.

The origins of Kasuga Taisha, the Fujiwara family shrine, are veiled in mystery. Presumably Fujiwara no Fubito enshrined the deity of Kashima here shortly after Nara became capital. A poem in the *Manyōshū* mentions the Kasuga Festival for which the shrine is

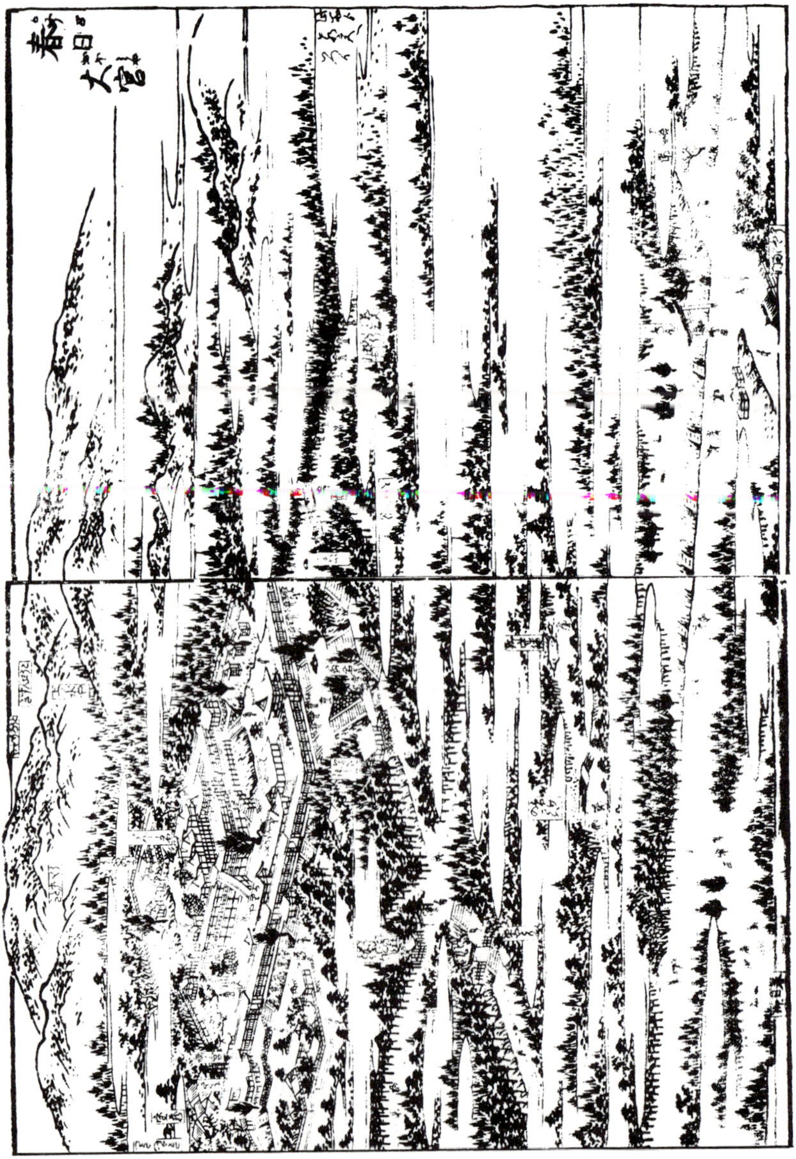

156

春日大宮

Kasuga Shrine (*Yamato Meisho-zue*)

famous, verifying that the shrine definitely existed in 751. Another Nara Period document states that in 768 three additional deities were transferred to the shrine to make a total of four.

The divinities enshrined at Kasuga Taisha raise a number of questions. Those in the First and Second Shrines of the complex are Takemikazuchi, who was transferred from Kashima Shrine (now southern Ibaragi Prefecture), and Futsunushi, from Katori Shrine (now northern Chiba Prefecture). Why did Fubito, a descendant of the Nakatomi clan long in service to the emperors as ritualists, enshrine these eastern frontier divinities as his ancestral deities? The answer probably lies in Japanese mythology. Takemikazuchi and Futsunushi were the deities who convinced the divinity of Izumo, Ōkuninushi (also Ōnamochi), to surrender to the Yamato state. In addition, it was Takemikazuchi who gave Jimmu the sword Futsu no Mitama (now enshrined at Isonokami Shrine) to assist him in his conquest of the local tribes of Kumano and Yamato. These deities were probably enshrined in the northern frontier of Yamato rule because of their "conquering powers" used in the subjugation of the eastern provinces (now roughly the Kantō Plain). By enshrining military deities that had been used in the conquest of new territories, Fubito may have been planning to bring more land under imperial rule.

Considering that the Fujiwara were descended from the Nakatomi, specialists in ritual, the deity in the Third Shrine, Ame no Koyane, is likely to be the ancestoral deity of the Fujiwara since, according to the *Kojiki* and *Nihon Shoki*, she was the deity sent to earth to take charge of liturgical matters. Ame no Koyane was initially enshrined at Hiraoka Shrine (in present-day Osaka) as was Hime, a minor deity, who was also transferred to Kasuga Shrine to become its fourth divinity.

Kasuga Taisha Shrine was established slightly uphill from the Fujiwara ancestral temple Kōfuku-ji, suggesting that Fubito may also have wished these deities to serve as protectors of the temple. After

158

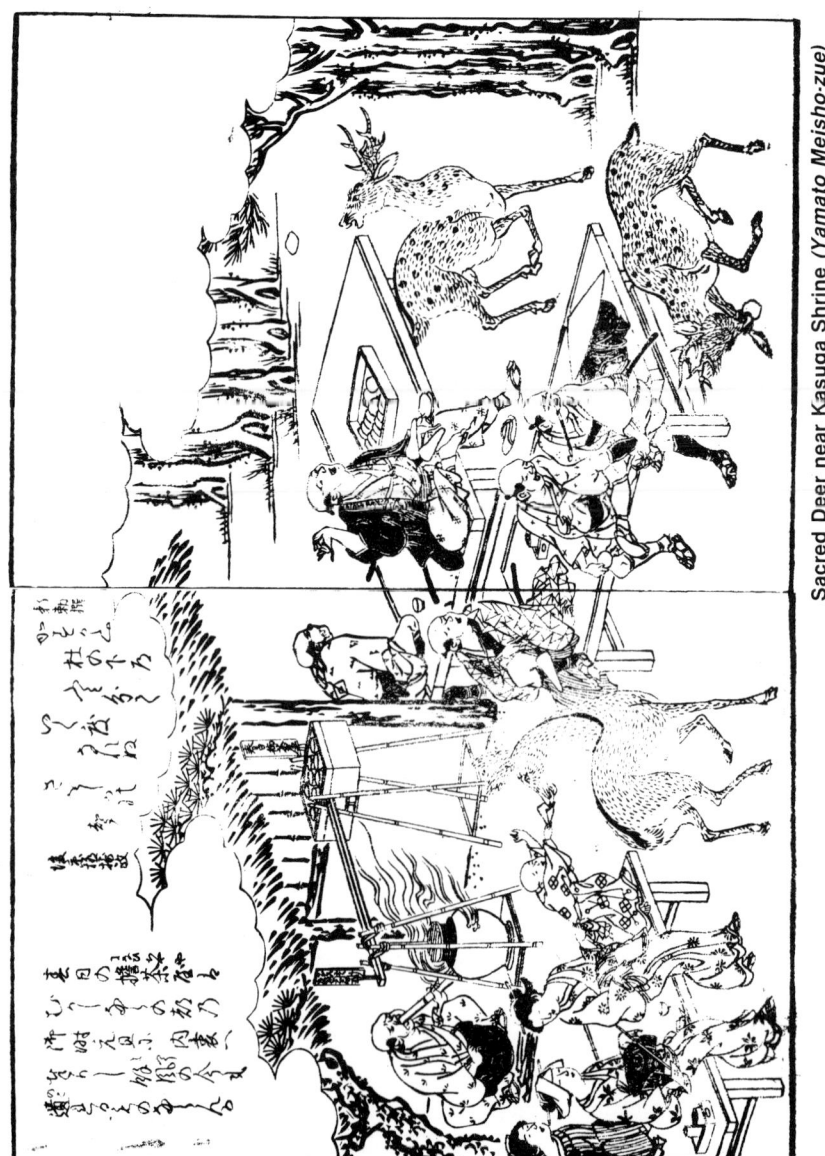

Sacred Deer near Kasuga Shrine (*Yamato Meisho-zue*)

Amaterasu, the Sun Goddess, gave her blessing to the foreign religion and showed herself willing to protect the Great Buddha of Nara, Shintō deities were often worshipped as temple guardians. Later Hachiman, a war deity possibly of Korean origin, was particularly depended on to fulfill this function and he was enshrined at Tamukeyama Hachiman-gū Shrine to protect the nearby Tōdai-ji Temple.

A map of Tōdai-ji that is preserved in the Shōsō-in Repository reveals that the area where Kasuga Shrine was built, mid-way up Mt. Mikasa (also known as Mt. Kasuga), was the sacred abode of local deities. The deer which freely roam the area symbolized the local deities and over the centuries came to be revered as the Fujiwara ancestors themselves. This is probably the reason why deer are kept at Kasuga Taisha as well as at all later Fujiwara ancestral shrines: Ōharano Shrine in Nagaoka when it was capital, then Yoshida Shrine in Kyoto when the capital was transferred there. It was forbidden to fell the trees of hallowed Mt. Kasuga, and it was an equally grave offense to slay a sacred deer.

Perhaps because of its role as protector of Kōfuku-ji Temple, Kasuga Taisha Shrine deities became amalgamated with Buddhas and bodhisattvas from the end of the Heian Period on when Shintō deities were often thought to be appearances of Buddhas and bodhisattvas. A number of mandalas issued from the synthesis and have become treasures of a peculiar Shintō-Buddhism art. In the *Kasuga Mandala*, drawn in 1309, the names of Buddhas and bodhisattvas are written in Sanscrit overtop of the four shrines of Kasuga. These mandalas grew out of the belief that the Kashima deity Takemikazuchi was the bodhisattva Fukūkenjaku Kannon; the Katori deity Futsunushi, the Buddha Yakushi; Ame no Koyane, the bodhisattva Jizō; and Hime, the Jūichimen (Eleven-headed) Kannon. Many such mandala were drawn. In the *Kasuga Shaji Mandala*, for example, Kasuga Shrine is drawn on the upper section and the Buddhist pantheon of Kōfuku-ji Temple on the lower half. The order is reversed in the *Kasuga Jōdo*

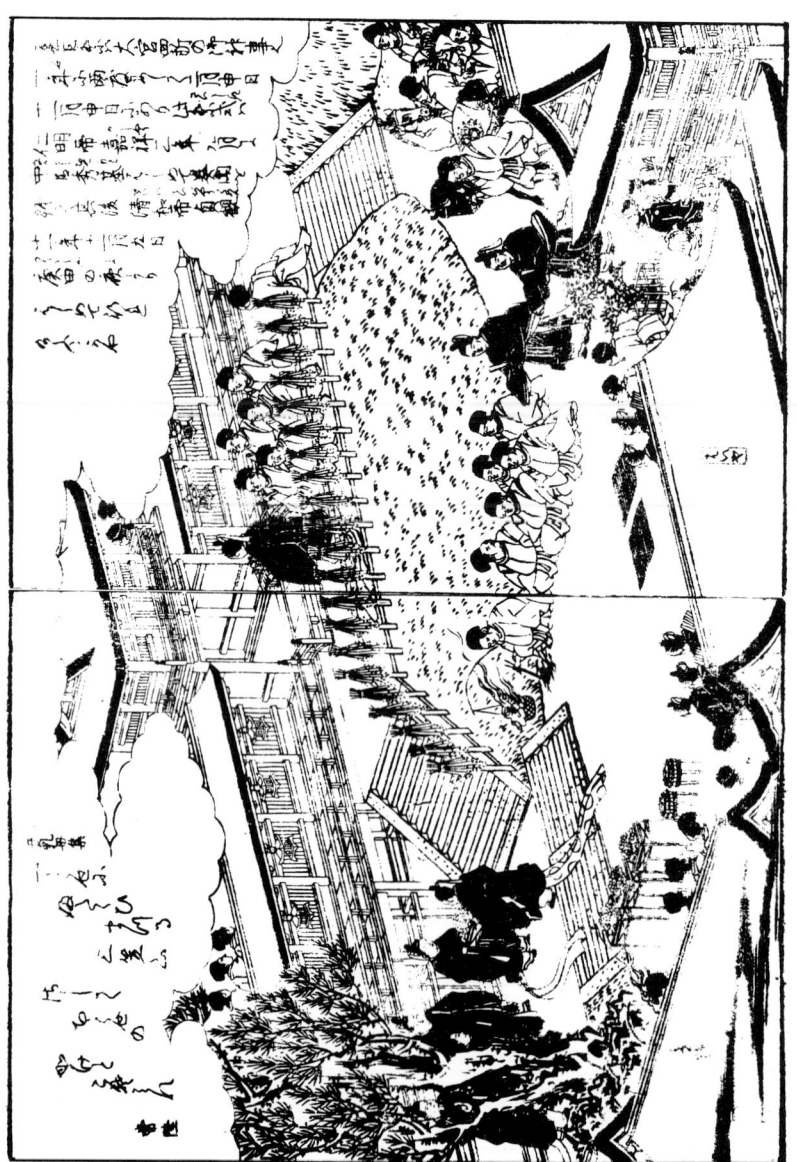

Kasuga Shrine Festival (Yamato Meisho-zue)

Mandala with Kasuga Shrine on the lower section and various Buddhas and bodhisattvas above sitting in front of paradisiacal temple halls. Sacred Mt. Mikasa is illustrated as the Buddhist Jōdo (Paradise). The *Kasuga Shika Mandala* is of special interest. Drawn in its center is a deer carrying on its saddle a sacred tree that is holding a mirror in its branches. Mirrors are the symbols of Shintō deities, and written on this one are the Sanscrit letters for the Buddhas and bodhisattvas from whom the Kasuga deities were believed to have derived. The mirror can also be interpreted as the full moon shedding light on the avenue that leads up to Kasuga Taisha Shrine.

The famous scroll entitled *Kasuga Gongen Reigen Ki* (Stories of the Miraculous Deeds of the Avatar of Kasuga), presented to the shrine in 1309, is also a record of the amalgamation of the two religions, of which Kasuga Taisha Shrine became a particularly strong exponent. It alludes to the closeness of the imperial and Fujiwara families by relating the Sun Goddess Amaterasu to the Kasuga deity Ame no Koyane. It then claims that Mt. Kasuga is equally holy as the Sacred Vulture Peak in India where Buddha delivered the sermon that became the *Lotus Sutra*, and that a pilgrimage to Kasuga Taisha Shrine is a path to salvation in no way inferior to a pilgrimage to the sacred places of Buddhism in India. One of the 58 miracles recounted in the scroll tells about a man who was promoted to a higher office and gained fortune and happiness by virtue of having presented prayers at the shrine. Stories such as these possibly encouraged pilgrimages to the shrine by others hoping that their religious needs or political ambitions would be fulfilled. They might also have contributed to the custom of donating stone and metal lanterns that still hang from shrine buildings and along the avenue leading up to them. These lanterns are one of the attractions of the shrine and are lit twice annually on February 3 and August 15.

Kasuga Taisha Shrine is famous for its colorful festivals held each year almost without interruption since the beginning of its eventful history. An atmosphere of courtly elegance and antiquity pervades the

162

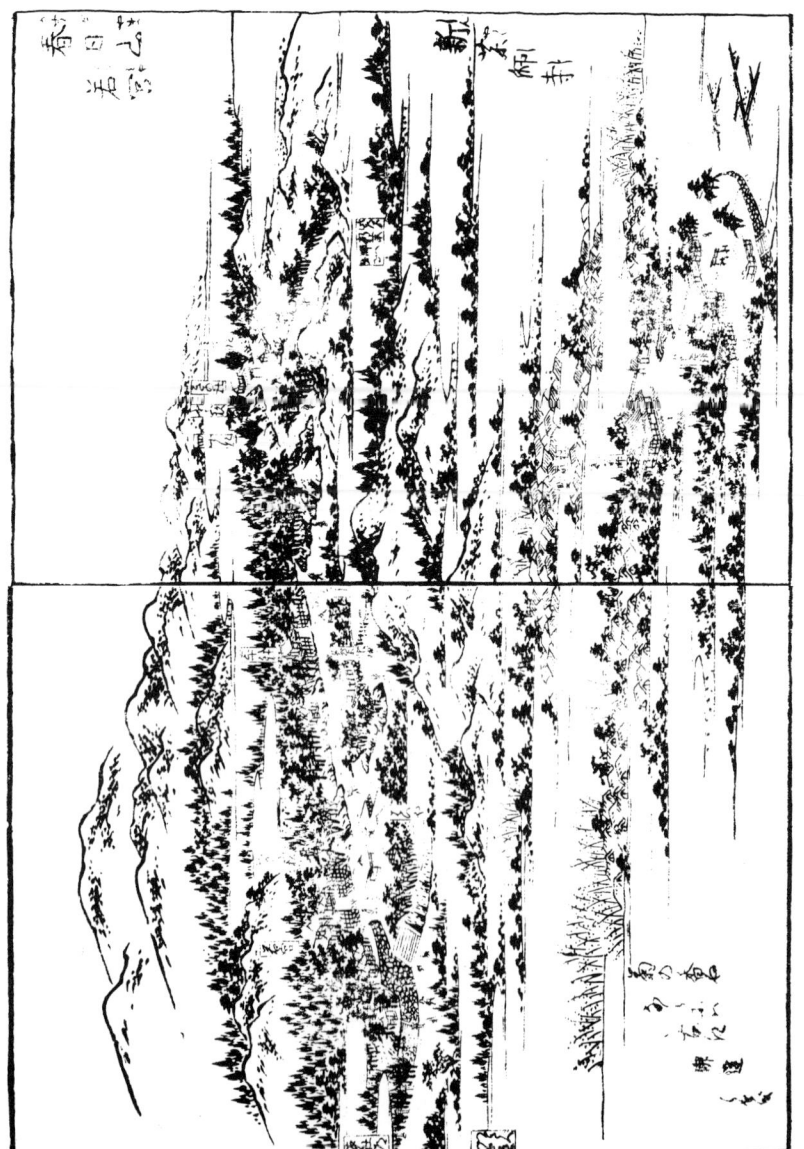

Wakamiya Shrine, Mt. Kasuga (Yamato Meisho-zue)

shrine when Bugaku dances of Chinese origin and Yamato-mai
(Yamato dances) are performed during the Kasuga Matsuri, one of the
Shrine's main ritual celebrations, on March 13. The custom of
selecting a female virgin member of the Fujiwara clan to serve the
Shrine and to be present at this festival was discontinued in the Heian
Period.

The Wakamiya Shrine and Shintō festivals: The major festival at
Kasuga Taisha is not connected with the shrine itself but with a sub-
shrine dedicated to the offspring of the deity Ame no Koyane; hence
its name Wakamiya, meaning "Young Shrine." The festival is simply
called On-matsuri, or Honorable Festival, but is in fact one of the
most spectacular festivals in the entire country. Watching the
festivities on December 17 and 18 one is taken on a journey back in
time to the remote past of Japan for the On-matsuri has been
performed annually according to tradition without interruption since
1136, the year after the shrine was erected. Although it incorporates
the cultural practices of China, Korea and Japan and the aristocratic
milieu of the Nara Period, it also consolidates the traditions of more
ancient Shintō festivals and therefore exemplifies early Shintō
celebrations in general.

Since we have already outlined the fundamentals of Buddhism,
the following discussion of Shintō festivals in general and of the On-
matsuri in particular will allow a better understanding of Japanese
culture and mentality and the various elements that contributed to
their formation.

As we have already seen, the conception of time marks one
fundamental difference between Buddhism and Shintō. The Buddhist
temples scattered about the Yamato Plain that were intended to be
permanent buildings — at least more permanent than Shintō
structures — symbolize the historical, linear system of time which the
Japanese adopted as part of the modernization of the state. Together
with this historical system of time, the ancient circular system has also

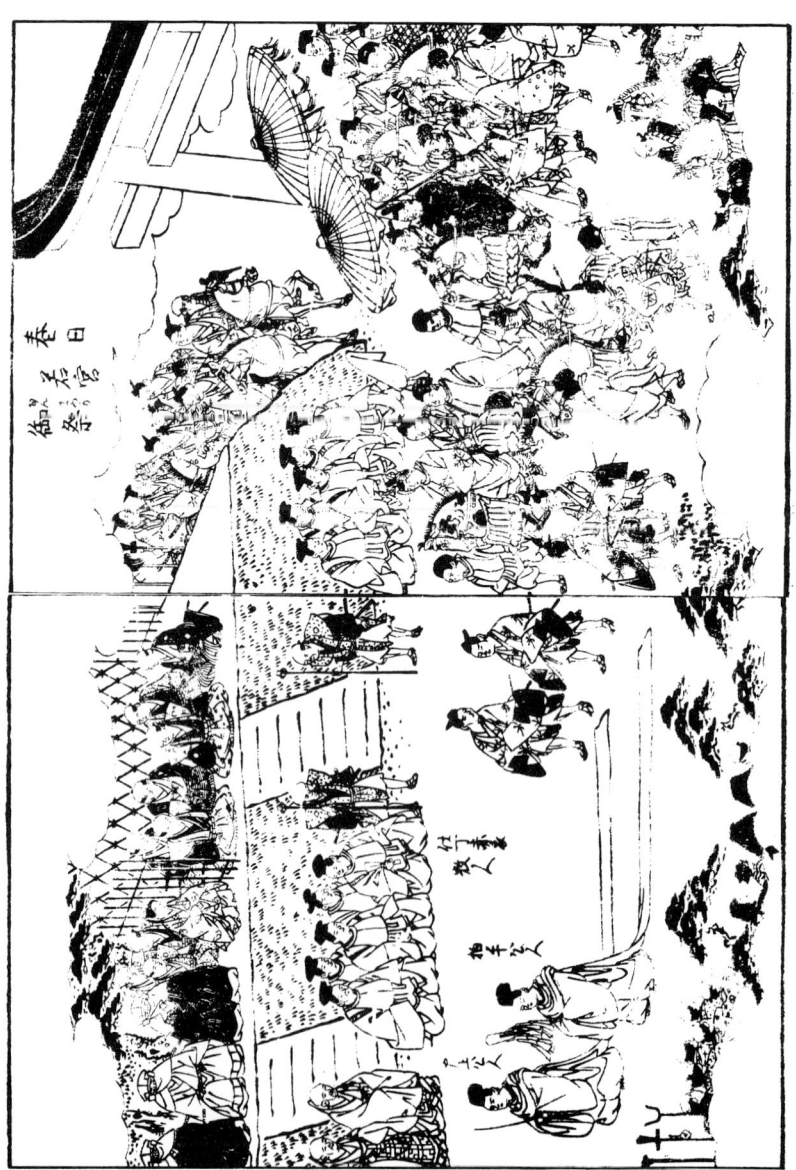

Wakamiya Shrine Festival *(Yamato Meisho-zue)*

survived into the present, especially in connection with the Shintō festivals. Such circular systems of time are based on the idea that time, rather than being irretrievable, comes to an end and must be renewed periodically after one or more years; hence the periodic rebuilding of Shintō shrines and the destruction and renewal of sacred objects one can still observe today at various Shintō rites throughout Japan. Periodic renewal is one of the key phrases to understanding Shintō.

The necessity to renew derived from the belief that by placating the local deities territories could be conquered or occupied, but that the placation was temporal and had to be repeated periodically. Deities had dual natures: *nigi,* the polished, orderly and peaceful aspect, and *ara,* the restless, mobile and chaotic disposition. Performing the renewal faithfully ensured the benevolence and protection of the territorial divinity which then exhibited its *nigi* nature and became peaceful and controllable. Failure to carry out the festivals rendered it wrathful and restless. Once a deity reverted to its *ara* nature, the territory and behavior of its inhabitants fell under its spell immediately and became ungovernable. It was therefore of the utmost importance that time be renewed for this ensured the continuation of order and civilization.

As well as being a religious, territorial, social and, of course, temporal act, renewal in Shintō was also political and agricultural. Time cycles began anew with the accession of each new emperor and the selection of a new capital. The cycle continued until the emperor's death or abdication and a new cycle entered with the enthronement of his successor. When permanent capitals were established, era names were given to the reign of each ruler and the number of years in that era were equal to the number of years he reigned. At his death a new era name was chosen for the reign of his successor and year one began again. The Japanese continue to use this system. So for example, the year 1983 is Shōwa 58 — the 58 referring to the 58 years that the Emperor Hirohito has reigned.

Agricultural renewal was equally important and probably

御旅所

Onmatsuri at Wakamiya Shrine, Kagura *(Nō no Zushiki)*

coexisted with the temporal and other forms of renewal. Unlike the sporadic political renewals, the agricultural versions were carried out regularly once a year. The On-matsuri was such a renewal. It was first held in an attempt to bring to an end a famine and epidemic in 1136.

Prayers and offerings of agricultural produce were two of the ritual means employed to appease the divinity and to renew time. Probably more important than these was artistic entertainment. If the deity was to be persuaded to continue its tolerance of interlopers on its land and to continue its agricultural beneficence, it had to be entertained. This was done by regaling it with various forms of art — music, dancing, poetry, storytelling, theatrical dramas and comedies. They were presented in front of the local deities rather than an audience because the strict order of each performance was thought to have magical power strong enough to placate the divinities.

The earliest example of art being used to placate a deity is recorded in the *Kojiki* in the myth of the Sun Goddess. Amaterasu was a peaceful deity until her brother, the Storm God Susanoo, destroyed the organization of her rice fields and disturbed the peace of her palace by throwing a horse onto her roof. Enraged, Amaterasu reverted to her *ara* nature. She hid herself in a cave causing darkness to envelop heaven and earth. To assuage her anger and to have her shine on the plains of heaven again, other deities assembled in front of the cave and entertained her with a striptease-like dance. Curious, Amaterasu finally emerged from the cave to investigate the merrymaking. Her light shone over the earth once more.

In its use of art, the On-matsuri was, and is, a typical festival aimed at pacifying the perturbed deity and thereby ensuring its continued benevolence and agricultural generosity. It was also hoped that having been well diverted, the deity would willingly return to its shrine and contentedly await the following year when the same festival would dutifully be repeated in faithful imitation of the past.

Like most Shintō festivals, the On-matsuri is divided into three distinct sections: *Kami-oroshi* (Deity Descent), *Kami-asobi* (Deity

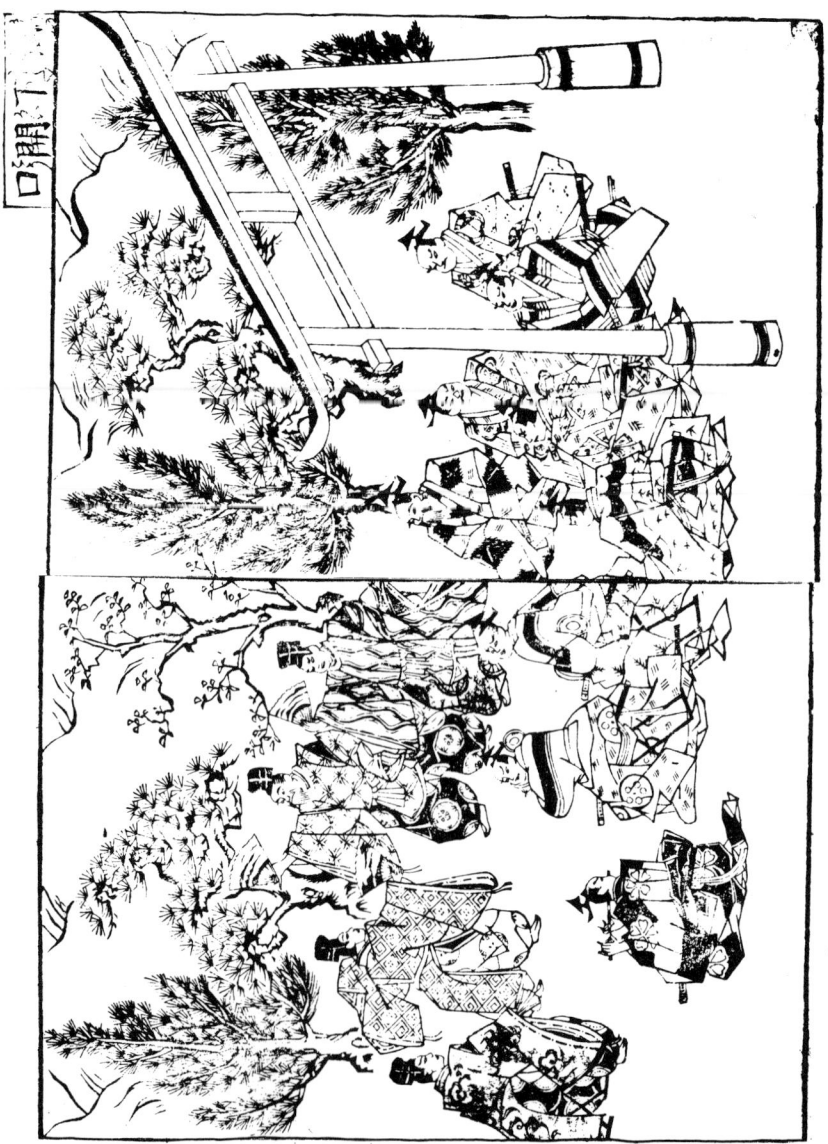

Onmatsuri at Wakamiya Shrine. Performance underneath the Yōgo Pine. *(Nō no Zushiki)*

Entertainment) and *Kami-okuri* (Deity Return). During *Kami-oroshi* the local deity is taken from the shrine at night time (the night of December 16) and carried down to the foot of Mt. Kasuga. This symbolizes the abolition of time and, in a sense, a return to chaos. At the foot of the mountain the deity is installed in a temporary shrine called *tabisho* (Travel [Resting] Place) and it is here, from a lawn stage in front of the *tabisho*, that the deity is entertained. *Kami-asobi* (this continues throughout December 17) deserves special attention because of its close association with various traditional arts.

A procession of dignitaries and artists proceeds from San-jō, or Third Street (the procession once left from Kōfuku-ji Temple), to the *tabisho*. En route, just past the first shrine gate, stands a pine called Yōgō-matsu. A legendary old man (okina) is said to have appeared under this tree once upon a time and started to dance. He was thought to be the Kasuga deity performing a dance called Manzai-raku or the Dance of Longevity. This became the prototype of Okina dances in Nō plays, (the highly formalized dramas developed in the 13th and 14th centuries) and the Yōgō-matsu tree is painted on the back wall of all Nō stages. The procession stops for a while beside this pine and representatives of the Komparu School of Nō (formerly the Kanze, Komparu, Hōshō and Kongō schools also took part), the Moriyama School of Kyōgen,* and Dengaku (Field Dances)** performers present prayers and perform in the same spot where the Okina once danced. These performances include Kaikō (Opening Mouth), a prologue or introductory performance in which the virtues of the deity are praised; a Yumiya Tachiawase, literally, a joining of bow and arrow (the bow

---

* Kyōgen developed out of comic imitations or mimicry of more serious, ritual dances such as Kagura or Okina. In Okina performances, Kyōgen actors wearing black masks performed the comic parodies called Sambasō. Kyōgen were incorporated into the Nō plays (Aikyōgen) but also developed into independent farcical plays.

** Dengaku was a precursor of the Nō plays that grew out of simple, rustic field dances and acrobatics.

170

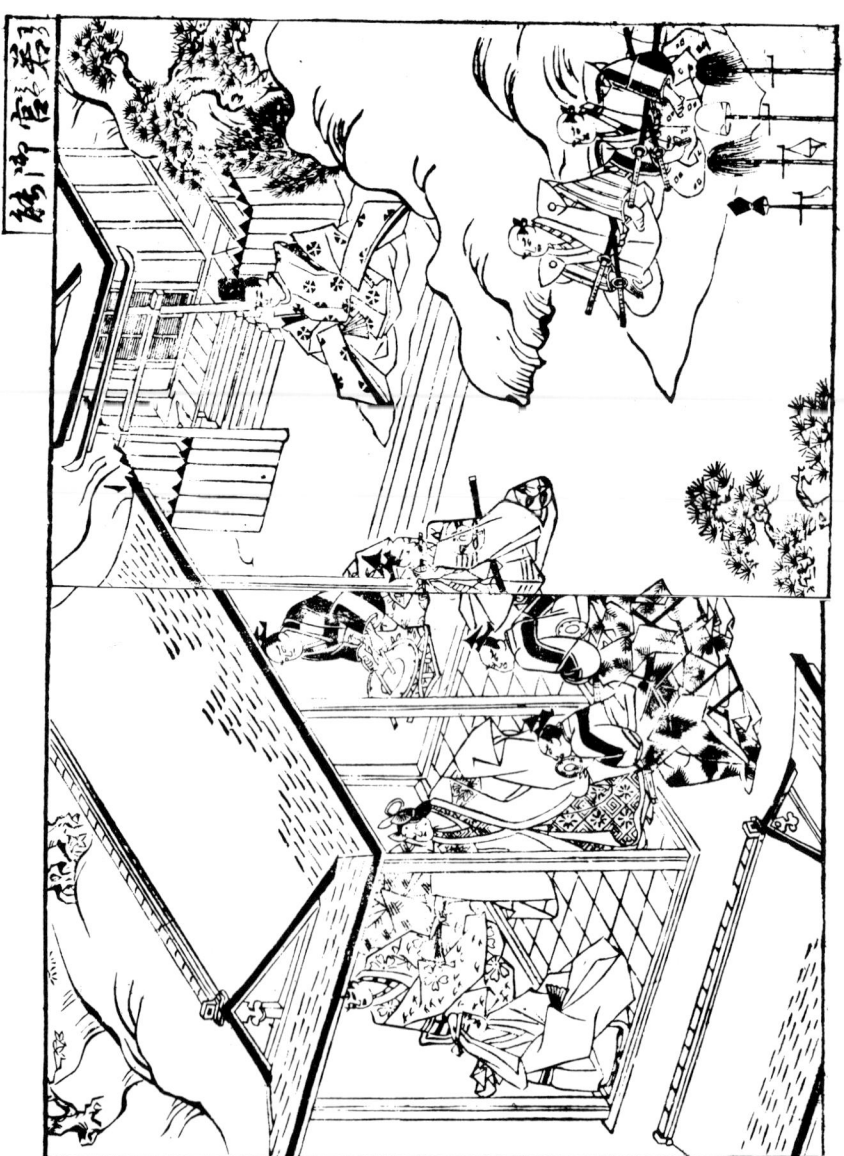

Onmatsuri at Wakamiya Shrine, Nō Play (Nō no Zushiki)

and arrow are symbols of deities and Buddhas, Yin and Yang and virtuous rule); a Mikasa Fūryū (a Kyōgen), an antique, auspicious dance during which congratulatory words are recited; and a piece of Dengaku formerly presented by semi-professional Dengaku priests attached to the Kōfuku-ji. The prime functions of these presentations is to ensure that the deity will continue to grant the earth with the gift of fertility and will enable the heads of these schools to maintain standards of excellence in their arts. In early Japan actors were shamans or media through whom deities, supernatural beings and even Buddhas and bodhisattvas were able to express themselves.

Once the procession reaches the *tabisho,* the shrine officials present offerings and prayers to the deity. This is followed by dances called Azuma-asobi and Kagura performed by virgins who serve the shrine. Azuma-asobi originated in Udo, Suruga Province (present Shizuoka Prefecture) where they were performed, it is said, by heavenly maidens descended to earth. Next is another performance of Dengaku danced by an actor dressed in a wisteria-patterned gown and waving a baton-like rod with many five-colored paper strips used for purification, streaming from it. Another Kaikō (Opening Mouth) follows this in which the deity's benevolence is analogized to the powers of the Buddhas. The recitations express appreciation for the deity's bestowal of happiness and abundant harvests.

After the Kaikō, a Seinō dance is performed by two men clad in white. Seinō were popular folk dances with elements of mimicry and realism that portrayed the feats of deities: for example Isora, a vassal of the sea god, holding high the magic balls that symbolize his power, and Kanju and Manju assisting the naval forces of Empress Jingū in her military campaign against Korea. The dances end and all is still. Suddenly the silence is broken by the loud beating of two huge drums. The drums, one representing the Sun, the other the Moon, stand at each side of the avenue that leads to the lawn stage. They announce the start of Bugaku, dances imported from China and Korea but which probably travelled to those countries from places as far away as

India and Burma. Actors dressed in Chinese robes dance to the accompaniment of Chinese Gagaku music that reached Japan in the Nara Period if not earlier.

The following is a list of the dances, primarily Bugaku, that are performed at the *tabisho*. Dances in which the first participant proceeds to the left of the stage are of Chinese origin and those where he proceeds to the right are Korean. The masks worn by the dancers symbolize supernatural beings, legendary kings and heroes.

1)   Embu Sansetsu

This is a short dance which opens the program of Bugaku and is presented as a prayer for the art itself. The dancers appear one by one on the stage waving their wooden halberds in three directions to purify the stage.

2)   Manzai-raku

(Left)   This dance originated in the Sui Dynasty, China, where it was performed at enthronement ceremonies to wish the newly installed emperor a long and prosperous life.

3)   Engi-raku

This follows a Korean pattern of dance but was actually created by Fujiwara no Tadafusa in the Engi Era (901-923).

4)   Katen

(Left)   Katen, a Japanese dance, was arranged to a T'ang China piece of music played on the biwa (a kind of lute). The dancers of this very graceful and elegant dance wear the costumes of civil servants.

5)   Chikyū

(Right)   The origins of this dance are obscure. It may have come from the Kingdom of Parhae (roughly, present Manchuria).

6)   Kagura-shiki

This is a simplified Okina dance performed by Komparu actors. The old man dressed in white represents the Sun Goddess, the man in black the Kasuga deity, and a third man called Chitose, the deity of Hachiman. They congratulate one another then promise to bestow longevity and rich, bountiful harvests. This is followed by a Sambasō dance in which a Kyōgen actor, a bell in his right hand and a fan in his left, mimics the Okina dance. This is traditionally performed prior to the Bugaku dances.

7) Yamato-mai

These dances, accompanied by song, were first performed in the fifth century in Yamato. Depending on the category, Yamato-mai can be presented by one to as many as eight dancers. Yamato-mai were also performed during imperial ceremonies such as Daijō-e and Chinkon-sai (placation of evil spirits).

8) Ranryō-ō

(Left)   This recounts the story of the Chinese King Chiang-kung of Lan-Ling (in Japanese, Ranryō) who was invincible in battle but always wore a ferocious mask to hide his gentle face from the enemy.

9) Nasori

(Right)   This is a jumping or "running" style dance that originated in Korea. It is also known as the Double Dragon Dance.

10) Sanju

(Left)   A dynamic war dance, it portrays a deity leading the army of Empress Jingū to victory over Korea.

11) Kitoku

(Right)   This dance is also of the "running" style and is performed by one dancer. Its origins are obscure.

12) Batō

(Left)   King Pedu of India is portrayed in this dance mounted on a white horse as he goes off to kill a poisonous snake. According to Shintō traditions, this dance may also portray Lao-tzu (6th century B.C.), the founder of Chinese Taoism, chasing away an angry beast.

13) Rakuson

(Right)   This is a one-man, *nasori* or running dance.

At Kasuga Shrine, all these cultural traditions from China and

Korea as well as from Japan were combined and came to be copied by the Imperial Court, Atsuta Shrine (Nagoya City) and Itsukushima Shrine (Miyajima, Hiroshima Prefecture) in their own festivals and celebrations. All these dances are striking in the very strict order with which they are performed. The movements when danced by more than one dancer are a picture of strict symmetrical coordination. The precision is deliberate for it was this very balance that was thought to hold the power to recreate time and social order over the territory as well as to assure its agricultural prosperity. It is not coincidental that many of the dances portray kings and heroes subduing enemies or beasts, or, in other words, chaos and disorder.

These performances (lasting from about 3 p.m. to 11 p.m.) bring to an end the Kami-asobi sequence and preparations are made to return the now appeased deity to its permanent shrine. *Kami-okuri*, the re-enshrining of the divinity, is carried out in total darkness, the road marked only by glowing ashes. Shintō priests surround the box in which the symbol of the deity is apparently kept as they carry it back to the Main Shrine of Wakamiya. After the re-enshrinement has been completed, two more Kagura are danced in front of the sanctuary. The following day (November 18th), performances of Nō plays and a sumo-wrestling match are held at the *tabisho*. Sumo is an old shrine ritual once used for divinatory purposes.

The dedication of these various dances before the Wakamiya *tabisho* undoubtedly deeply influenced their development and preservation. This festival has had a particular impact on the cultivation of the Nō theater. The Nō stages are said to be replicas of the lawn stage in front of the *tabisho*. And it is thanks to the sponsorship of professional dancers, musicians and actors by both Kasuga Shrine and Kōfuku-ji Temple that these arts have matured and survived until modern times.

SAIDAI-JI TEMPLE AND THE END OF NARA

Ironically, the cause of Nara's decline was the very religion with which the emperor sought to establish the city as a permanent capital. The close parallelism of Buddhism and state however could not be sustained. As we have seen, the charisma of the Japanese emperors depended primarily upon their fulfillment of certain religious functions and their preservation of ritual cleanliness, both of which had their roots in archaic Shintō. With the establishment of Buddhism as a state religion, the Buddhist priesthood assumed many of the ancient religious prerogatives of the emperors and so encroached upon the very basis of their authority. One of the major forces behind this development was the early synthesis of Shintō and Buddhism in which the latter was often considered as superior to the other. Shintō deities came to be seen as mere incarnations or later appearances of the Buddhas and bodhisattvas; thus the Buddhas were established as the sources of everything, including the ancestry of the imperial family. The close tie between temples and state resulted in a relationship between an emperor-priest, so to speak, and the Buddhist priesthood so close that by the end of the Nara Period the emperor was confronted by the threat of usurpation.

The hazardous association between the two became conspicuously apparent at the end of the Nara Period when the priest Dōkyō (d. 772) became particularly intimate with the Empress Kōken (r. 749-758 and 764-770). Their story begins with the rebellion of Fujiwara no Nakamaro (706-764). Nakamaro had a remarkable career. Upon attaining the Prime Ministership, the highest office under the throne, he delegated his children to key government posts and became virtually indomitable. His power remained unchallenged until the Empress Kōken fell under the influence of Priest Dōkyō. Aware of the threat the priest posed to his hegemony, Nakamaro ordered some of the troops that had been reserved for an attack on Korea to carry out a coup d'etat in 764. Nakamaro was betrayed and forced to flee. When

176

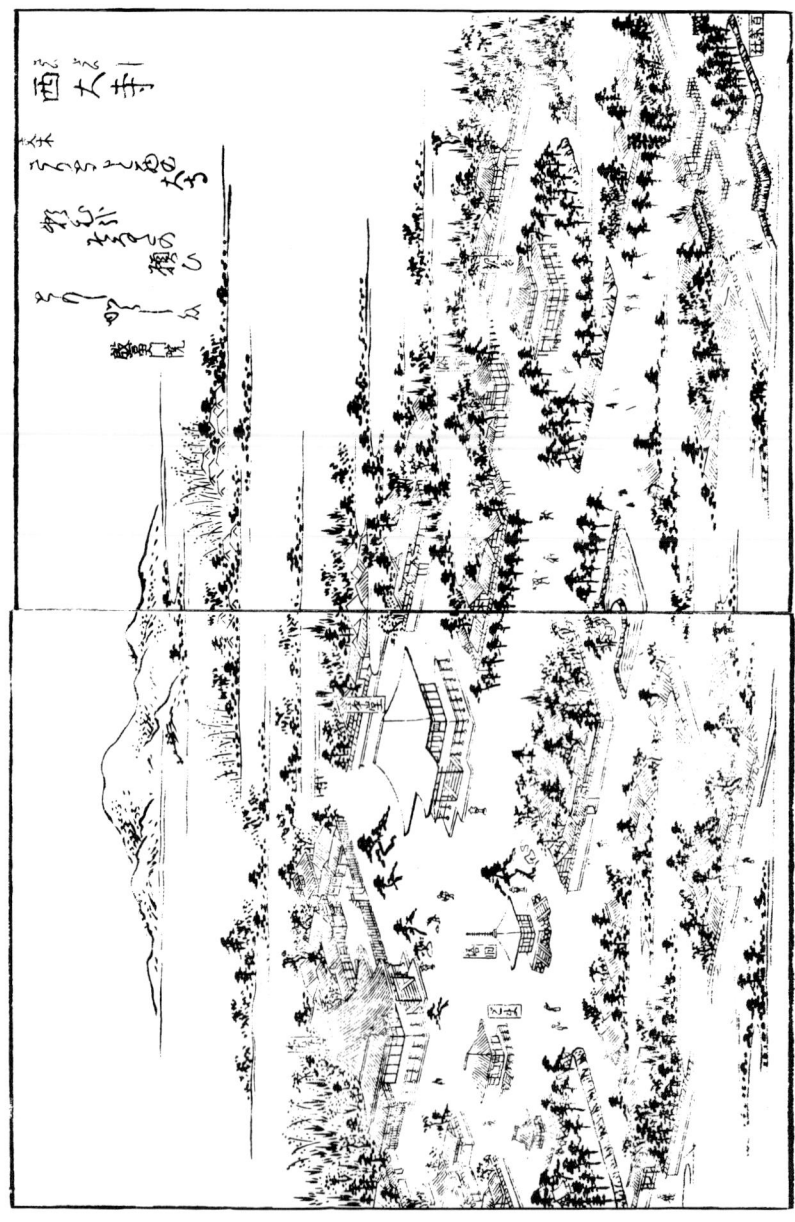

Saidai-ji Temple (*Yamato Meisho-zue*)

he was caught, he, his wife and his children were put to death.

Who was this priest Dōkyō under whose dominance the Empress fell? In his youth, he had undergone austerities on Mt. Katsuragi. After descending from the mountains he gained a reputation as a magical healer and when Empress Kōken became sick in 761, he was summoned to her side. Dōkyō readily cured her, and in recognition of his healing powers, he was made a Lesser High Priest in 763. This gave him greater access to the Empress who fell increasingly under his spell.

The following year, as a prayer for the subjugation of Nakamaro's rebellion, the Empress had Dōkyō cast copper and gold statues of the Four Heavenly Kings who it was hoped would quell the foes of the state in the same manner as they trampled upon demons. A year later, Saidai-ji Temple was built to shelter them. Tōdai-ji Temple already flanked the eastern side of the imperial palace. To complete the symmetry four blocks were made available for Saidai-ji on the western side.

The two Kondō (Main Halls) were massive structures only slightly smaller than the Daibutsu-den at Tōdai-ji. One was dedicated to the Buddha Yakushi and the other to Miroku (the former built for Kōken, the latter for Dōkyō) in a symbolic act to marry Yakushi of the present world with Miroku of the future world. A cloister connected both halls with the Chūmon (Middle Gate). The two five-storied pagodas of Saidai-ji, which stood to the south of Chūdaimon (Middle Great Gate) and to the left and right of the central avenue, rose higher even than the Tōdai-ji's pagoda. It was intended to have been higher still. According to the Nihon Ryōiki (Miraculous Stories from the Japanese Buddhist Tradition) Fujiwara no Nagate was condemned to hell for reducing the planned seven-storied pagoda by two stories and for erecting a square rather than an octagonal structure.

The Nihon Ryōiki also recounts the far from spiritual relationship that existed between Dōkyō and Empress, who after the quelling of

Nakamaro's rebellion reassumed the throne under the name of
Shōtoku.

Also in the reign of the empress dowager there was a
song which circulated among the people in the country:

> Don't be contemptuous of monks because of their robes.
> For under their skirts are hung garters and hammers.
> When the hammers erect themselves,
> The monks turn out to be awesome lords.
>
> . . . .

In the reign of Empress Abe [Shōtoku], in the beginning
of the second year of the snake, the first year of the Tempyō
jingo era, Dharma Master Dōkyō of the Yuge family had
intercourse with the empress on the same pillow, hearing the
affairs of state and ruling over the country together. The
above songs were a prediction of his relations with the
empress and his control over state affairs.

Also in the reign of the empress dowager, there was a
song that went like this:

> Look straight at the root of the tree,
> And you will find the most venerable master
> Standing satiated and fat.

It is evident that this was a prediction of the participation in
state affairs of Dharma Master Dōkyō as Dharma King . . . .

(Transl. by Kyoko Motomochi Nakamura)

Dōkyō's ambitions did not end there. He sought through the
pronouncement of an oracle to ascend the throne himself, but a
subsequent divination discredited the original oracle. With the death
of Empress Shōtoku, Dōkyō fell into disrepute and was banished from
the capital. He died soon after. To the imperial family and the
aristocracy, the Dōkyō affair signaled the danger the Buddhist
priesthood presented to the throne and in 784 the imperial family and

the aristocracy decided to transfer the capital away from the influence of the Nara temples. In doing so they overcame one of the gravest crises the throne had ever had to confront.

Despite the discreditation of Dōkyō, the Saidai-ji was not abandoned after the affair, although it was left unfinished. After a fire in 1140, only a refectory, a pagoda and the hall dedicated to the Four Heavenly Kings remained. These halls too would have fallen into disrepair were it not for Eison (d. 1290), one of the most energetic Saidai-ji priests, who was deeply involved in the reconstruction of temples in the twelfth century. Eison converted the Saidai-ji into a temple of the Shingon Sect. Dainichi, the central Buddha, was the focus of worship in Shingon and it was on the basis of the *Dainichi-kyō* Sutra that had been presented to Empress Kōken and was preserved at Saidai-ji that he wished to make the conversion. Being a true medieval Japanese eclectic, Eison also planned to combine Shingon with Ganjin's Ritsu sect. To bring the latter to Saidai-ji, he had a copy made of the Buddha Shaka at Seiryō-ji Temple in Kyoto. Eison is still remembered today at Saidai-ji where a tea ceremony is held in his memory on the second Sunday of October each year. The utensils used are of unusual size making the ceremony somewhat comic. Perhaps it was because of Empress Shōtoku's close relations to Saidai-ji which she helped to erect, that her tomb was built just north of the temple at a place from where one can gain a clear view of its grounds.

Saidai-ji waned in vitality after the transfer of the capital away from Nara and after the death of Priest Eison. However this did not prevent Saidai-ji monks from claiming that the Kamikaze (Divine Wind) which averted the two Mongol attacks on Japan in 1274 and 1281 was a product of the special prayers they had offered at Saidai-ji. The temple was razed in a blaze in 1502 and though it was partially rebuilt during the Edo Period, it never regained its original splendor.

NARA: ITS HISTORIES AND LITERATURE

In earlier days, the keeping of records was the duty of a clan of professional reciters who memorized important facts and decisions and passed them on orally from generation to generation. When Japan began to assimilate aspects of Chinese civilization and entered into relations with Korea and China, however, the ability to keep written documents became desirable. Writing was first entrusted to official scribes, who were often immigrants or their descendants and so were familiar with the Chinese language and script, which at that time was the international language of the Far East.

The necessity for a more literate officialdom had emerged from the thorough social and political reorganization of the new state. When the concept of historical time was adopted it became impossible for the government to function properly without documenting on paper its daily procedures and major events in the life of the nation. These documents were intended to help later generations compile histories and to learn from and imitate the past. Since precedence had become so highly esteemed, the recording of history became an integral facet of state affairs. The keeping of records and the compilation of histories was learned from the Chinese who considered history to be the very core of civilization. For the Chinese, the Golden Age lay in the irretrievable past — hence the necessity to emulate what had gone before by following documented precedence. For the Japanese, however, during a time when their country was being submerged in Chinese civilization, the retracing and chronicling of their past comprised a pris de conscience on the part of Japan as a nation.

The writing of a history was also necessitated by other factors. In order for emperors to centralize the country and to impose their will on the local clans, it was essential that they demonstrate the divine and mythical superiority of the imperial ancestors over those of other clans. Only by establishing the prepotency of the Sun Goddess Amaterasu could they assert a divine right to rule over all of Japan. An official history of the nation based on the imperial family and its ancestral deities would support and legitimize their claim to divine right.

This issue coincided with another problem, that of the ancestral mythology of other powerful families. Following the Jinshin War of 672, one of the many fierce succession struggles, the victorious Emperor Temmu, in an effort to claim legitimacy for the emperors and so avoid similar strife in the future, ordered the compilation of a history saying:

> "I hear that the chronicles of the emperors and likewise the original words in the possession of the various families deviate from the exact truth and are mostly amplified by empty falsehoods. If at the present time these imperfections be not amended, ere many years shall have elapsed, the purport of this, the great basis of the country, the grand foundation of the monarchy, will be destroyed. So now I desire to have the chronicles of the emperors selected and recorded, and the old words examined and ascertained, falsehoods being erased and truth determined, in order to transmit [the latter] to after ages."
>
> (Chamberlain, transl. *Kojiki*)

Temmu's concern that family histories be revised also stemmed from the difficulty in judging the validity of the claims of various clans for distinction and rank. These questions were determined by consideration of birth, ancestry and degree of relationship to the imperial family. Deliberate falsifications were inevitable rendering the emperor simply unable to take seriously all these claims, even though some might have been legitimate.

In order to compile the authoritative history, the compiler, Ō no Yasumaro (d. 723), depended on the extraordinary memory of one Hieda no Are. He was a member of a clan of reciters whose duty it was prior to the widespread introduction of writing, to memorize information, and he had probably memorized all the myths and annals of the imperial family. Records compiled into a history under the direction of Prince Shōtoku were also referred to. These had been stored in Soga no Umako's former residence but fortunately were saved from the flames when it burnt down during the Taika coup d'etat. Other sources used were the repertoire of ancient songs and dances performed by court musicians, popular legends, beliefs and rites, stories explaining the origin of place names, accounts of foreign origin and traditions of other families such as the Nakatomi, Mononobe and the Sarume, to whom Hieda no Are was related. Emperor Temmu died in 686 and did not live to see the culmination of this project. It was not until the reign of Empress Gemmyō in 712 that what was to become known as the *Kojiki* was completed.

The *Kojiki* was divided into a number of sections. It opened with the cosmogony and theogony myths then proceeded to give an account of all the monarchs beginning with Jimmu and ending with the death of Empress Suiko in 641. Beyond being an invaluable source of information on ancient Japan, it was primarily an attempt to justify the rule of the imperial family by subordinating other families and by downgrading the ancestral deities of clans in relation to the divine ancestors of the sovereigns. The deities of Izumo, a long time rival of Yamato, were particularly minimized. At the same time, the *Kojiki* was a compromise as was the new state itself. The heads of powerful families and long-established clans were incorporated into the new society of aristocrats by being assigned various official positions. Likewise, by stating in the *Kojiki* the relationship of their deities and ancestors to the imperial family's, the clans were granted hereditary rights under the new system to serve the emperors as officials. They were ranked in accordance with their importance vis-a-vis the imperial family as had been clarified in the new history.

Two years after the completion of the *Kojiki,* Empress Gemmyō gave orders for the preparation of a national history. The end product was the *Nihon Shoki* (Annals of Japan, also *Nihongi*), submitted to her in the year 720. Once again the compiler was Ō no Yasumaro. It was written entirely in Chinese (the *Kojiki* was written in Japanese) and records the years up to Empress Jitō's death in 697. The *Nihon Shoki*, compiled according to Chinese principles of historiography, was a considerably more coherent history and could be shown with pride to any foreign ambassador. National prestige demanded the writing of an authoritative history to establish the legitimacy of the imperial family in the eyes of the Chinese. This could only be achieved through demonstration of its antiquity, a Chinese concept. Consequently the *Nihon Shoki* attributes its early emperors with unnaturally long life spans. One hundred years of age or so was not uncommon. Nevertheless, compared with the *Kojiki*, it is a more reliable source especially of the less ancient history. Even so, taking either source at face value is hazardous since both histories are patchwork attempts to bring together various traditions of various provenances, and are in places of doubtful authenticity. In order to estimate the approximate date of the beginning of Yamato archaeological evidence must also be taken into account. The *Nihon Shoki* claims that Yamato goes back to sixth century B.C., whereas in actuality Jimmu's victory probably came in the third or fourth century A.D. Another problem, a frequent subject of scholarly discussion in post-war Japan, is whether the first ten emperors, beginning with Jimmu, are fictitious. In this case archaeological evidence points to the contrary and suggests that both the *Kojiki* and *Nihon Shoki* accurately list the number of Yamato emperors, that is to say those in line with the present imperial family, up to the date of their compilation.

Most of the ancient Japanese writings were in Chinese, often penned by Chinese or Korean scribes. The *Nihon Shoki,* for instance, was written entirely in Chinese, a script the Japanese, especially the educated male members of the upper classes, continued to use until recent times. In the *Kojiki,* however, because of its poems and passages of dialogue, the compilers were forced to use Chinese not ideographically but phonologically to represent Japanese sounds. Of course, this was nothing new to the Chinese language which, because of the introduction of Buddhism and its contacts with foreign tribes, had a number of Chinese graphs ready for phonetic reproduction of foreign sounds. This fact made it possible for the Japanese to use Chinese characters both as ideographs and as phonetic symbols. This they did in the *Kojiki*. That the Japanese could adapt the Chinese writing system to their own language indicates their genius in absorbing efficiently the cultural materials of more advanced nations without losing their own identity as a highly unique culture.

The use of the Chinese writing system for Japanese sounds made it possible to write entirely in the Japanese language. The first examples of this may be the poems inscribed on the Buddha's Footprint Stone at Yakushi-ji Temple. This system was used again in the mid-eighth century to compile the *Manyōshū* (Collection of Myriad Leaves), the first anthology of Japanese poetry. The motive behind the compilation of the *Manyōshū* must again be found in Japan's adoption of Chinese civilization in the Nara Period. In China, the compilation of anthologies had developed early and became, like the writing of history, a requisite for an advanced society. In all probability the Japanese had seen or heard of the *Shih Ching* (Book of Songs) said to have been compiled by Confucius (both the *Manyōshū* and the *Shih Ching* begin with a poem by an emperor), the *Chu Tsu,* compiled toward the end of the first century B.C. and the *Wen Hsuan,* a collection of Chinese poetry and prose penned between 221 B.C. and A.D. 502.

Some of the poems in the *Manyōshū*, 4,516 in total, go back as far as the reign of Emperor Yūryaku. These had possibly been memorized by court musicians or reciters and passed on orally until they were eventually committed to paper. The range of poems in the anthology marks the transition from primitive folk songs to elaborate expressions of joy or sorrow. They democratically include poems by emperors and also songs by peasants, frontier guards and women. Kakinomoto no

Hitomaro, Ōtomo no Yakamochi and Yamanoue no Okura were among the most prominent poets in the anthology. Together with the *Kojiki* and *Nihon Shoki,* the *Manyōshū* is a precious source enlightening us today on early Japanese religion and customs, emotions, attitudes towards life and death, wives, children and nature. The simplicity and sincerity of many of its poems have often been imitated by later generations of poets but never surpassed.

With the compilation of these histories and of the poetic heritage, Nara laid in place another important foundation stone of Japanese civilization. These compiling efforts were not soon forgotten but, on the contrary, served as an impetus for later generations of historiographers and poets to imitate the excellence of these pioneering works. Much of what we know today about early Japan came down to us thanks to the will of the Nara Period Japanese to record the past and to transmit it to the future.

*   *   *

When the Nara capital was abandoned in 784, the palace and other public and private buildings were dismantled and transported to the new capital at Nagaoka. But Nara did not disappear entirely. The temples, forbidden to follow the capital to Nagaoka as they had done when the capital was removed from Fujiwara to Nara, were forced to remain behind. Around about them grew up a *monzen-machi,* or temple city where accommodation was provided for pilgrims. Out of this evolved the modern city of Nara. The Nara priests continued to have a voice in politics in later periods, a direct outcome of which was the razing of the Nara temples by Taira no Shigehira in 1180. About 20 years after the capital was relocated in Kyoto, Emperor Heizei (r. 806-809) considered re-establishing the capital in Nara, but this project came to naught. Most probably economic reasons made any further such transferrals of capitals difficult if not impossible. The capitals had grown too large to be transferred elsewhere.

Nara is remembered for the political, religious and cultural foundations it laid for the development of Japan. Nor can its contributions to Japanese civilization in the fields of literature, art and architecture be overlooked. Though Nara as capital only for a brief seventy-odd years failed in its intended mission to become Japan's permanent capital, its impact on the subsequent evolution of the nation was so profound that it can indeed be called Japan's "permanent capital."

MAPS

in and around Nara

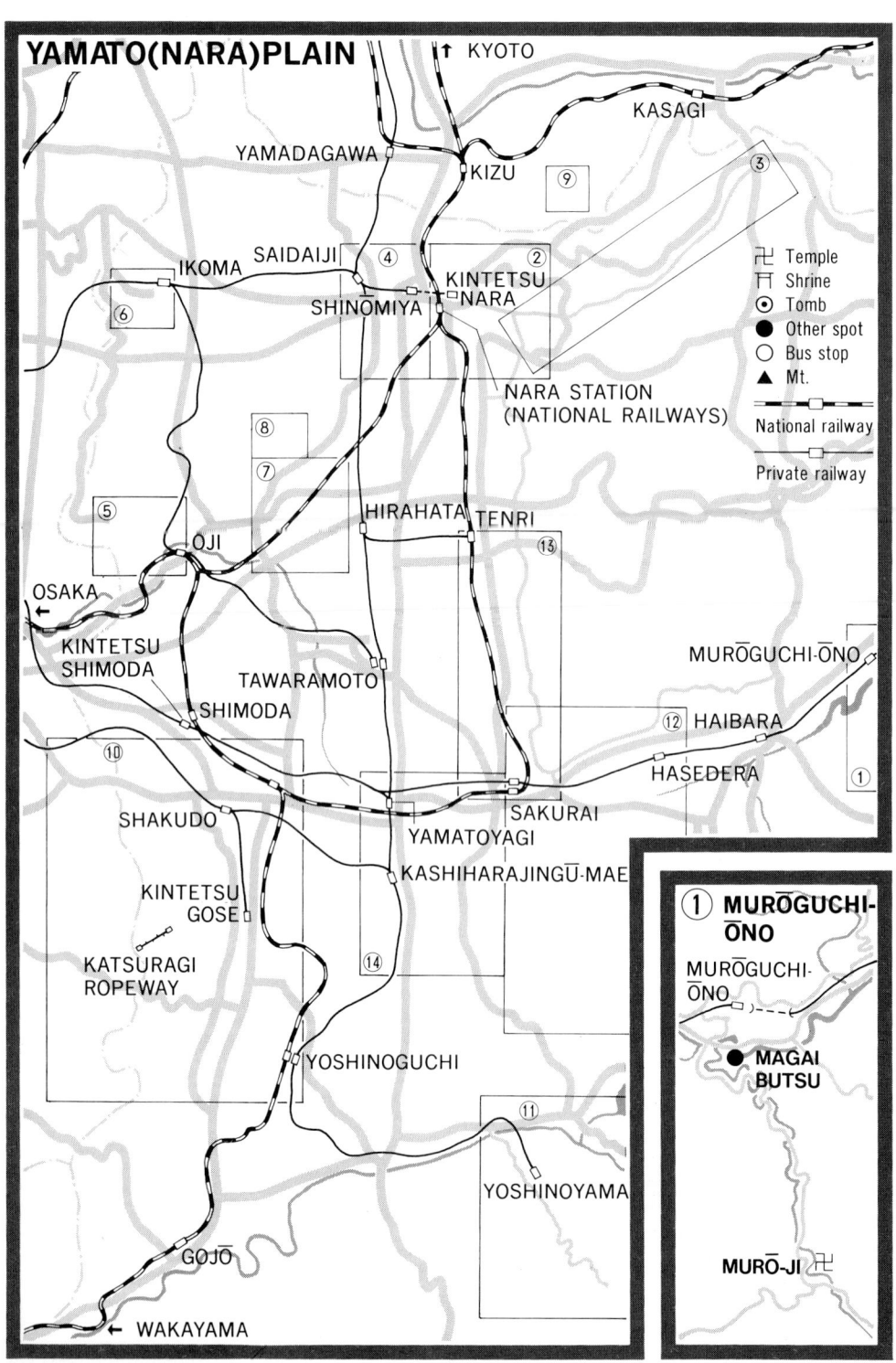

② NARA(EAST)

卍 HANNYA-JI

MT. MIKASA ▲

● JŪHACHIKEN-DŌ HOSPITAL

卍 FUTAI-JI

TENGAI-MON ●

卍 SHŌSŌ-IN

DAIBUTSU-DEN

NIGATSU-DŌ 卍

KAIDAN-IN 卍 卍

MT. ▲ WAKAKUSA

SANGATSU-DŌ 卍

鳥 TŌDAI-JI TAMUKEYAMA HACHIMAN SHRINE

KINTETSU NARA

NANDAI-MON ●

卍 HOKUENDŌ

NANENDŌ 卍 ● PAGODA

● TABISHO

鳥 KASUGA SHRINE

NARA STATION

KŌFUKU-JI

SARUSAWA POND

KASUGA WAKAMIYA 鳥 SHRINE

卍 GOKURAKU-BŌ

GANGŌ-JI 卍 卍 JŪRIN-IN

SHINYAKUSHI-JI 卍

BYAKUGŌ-JI 卍

KYŌBATE

卍 DAIAN-JI

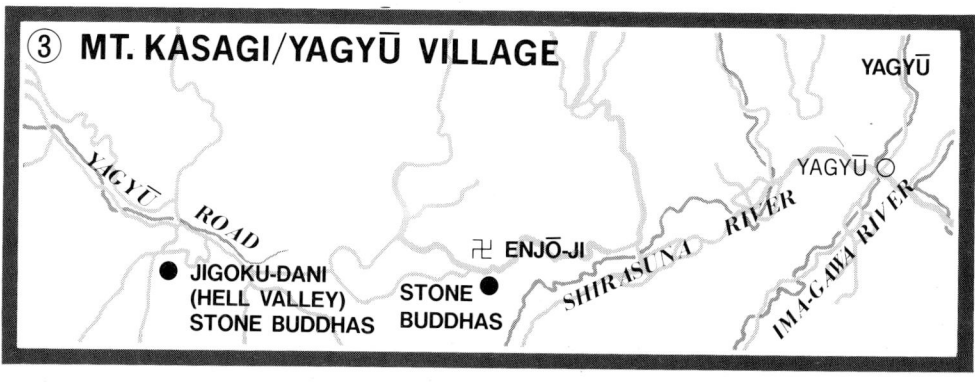

③ MT. KASAGI/YAGYŪ VILLAGE

YAGYŪ

YAGYŪ ROAD

YAGYŪ ○

卍 ENJŌ-JI

SHIRASUNA RIVER

IMA-GAWA RIVER

● JIGOKU-DANI (HELL VALLEY) STONE BUDDHAS

STONE ● BUDDHAS

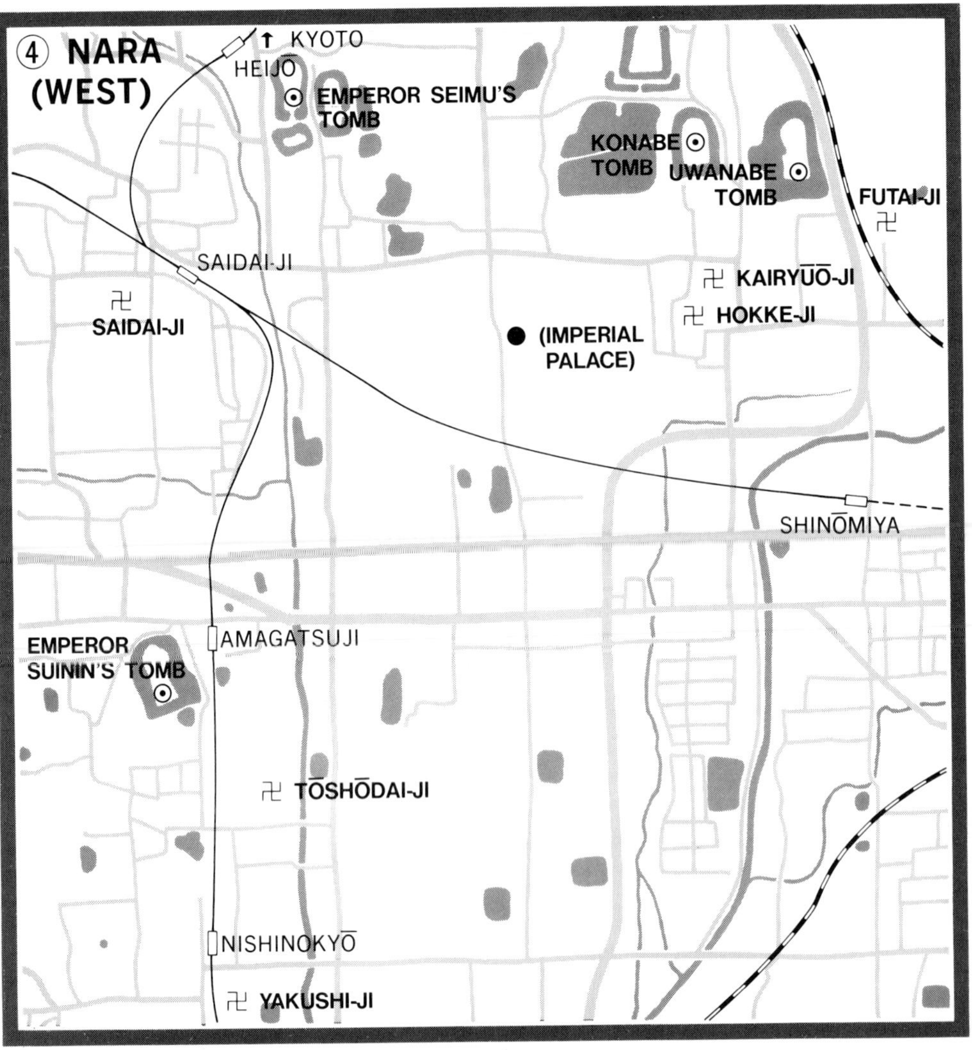

④ NARA (WEST)

↑ KYOTO

HEIJŌ

⊙ EMPEROR SEIMU'S TOMB

KONABE TOMB ⊙

UWANABE ⊙ TOMB

FUTAI-JI 卍

SAIDAI-JI

卍 SAIDAI-JI

卍 KAIRYŪO-JI

卍 HOKKE-JI

● (IMPERIAL PALACE)

SHINŌMIYA

EMPEROR SUININ'S TOMB ⊙

AMAGATSUJI

卍 TŌSHŌDAI-JI

NISHINOKYŌ

卍 YAKUSHI-JI

⑤ MT. SHIGISAN

TATSUTAGAWA

MT. SHIGISAN ▲ 卍

SHIGI-SAN

SEYA KITAGUCHI

BISHAMON-DŌ

SHIGISAN SHITA

TATSUTA TAISHA SHRINE 鳥

ŌJI

SANGŌ

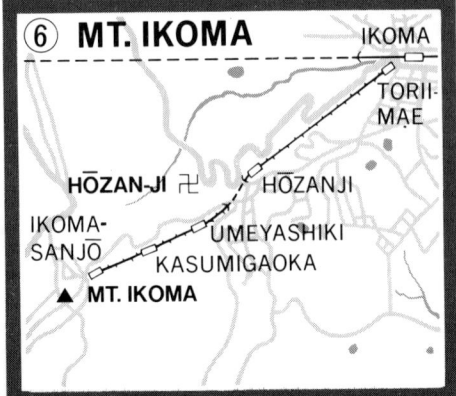

⑥ MT. IKOMA

IKOMA

TORII-MAE

HŌZAN-JI 卍

HŌZANJI

IKOMA-SANJŌ

UMEYASHIKI

KASUMIGAOKA

▲ MT. IKOMA

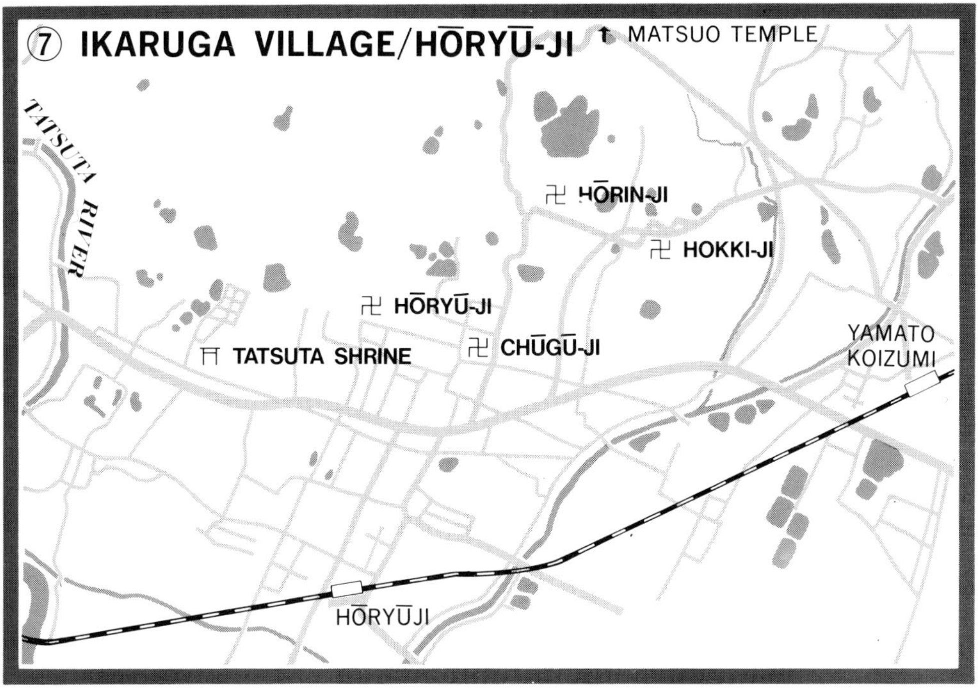

⑦ IKARUGA VILLAGE/HŌRYŪ-JI

↑ MATSUO TEMPLE

TATSUTA RIVER

卍 HŌRIN-JI

卍 HOKKI-JI

卍 HŌRYŪ-JI

鳥 TATSUTA SHRINE

卍 CHŪGŪ-JI

YAMATO KOIZUMI

HŌRYŪJI

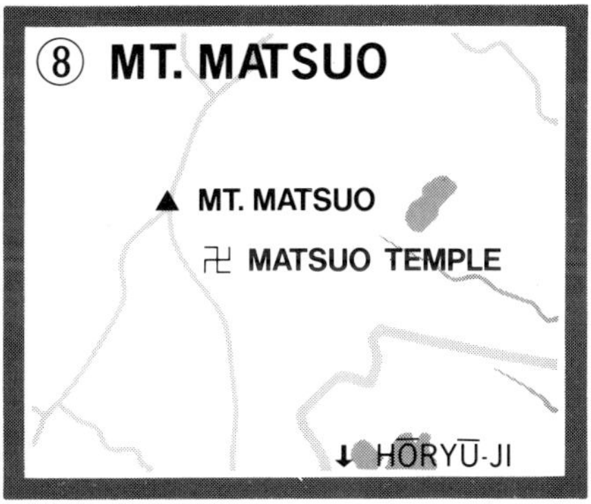

⑧ MT. MATSUO

▲ MT. MATSUO

卍 MATSUO TEMPLE

↓ HŌRYŪ-JI

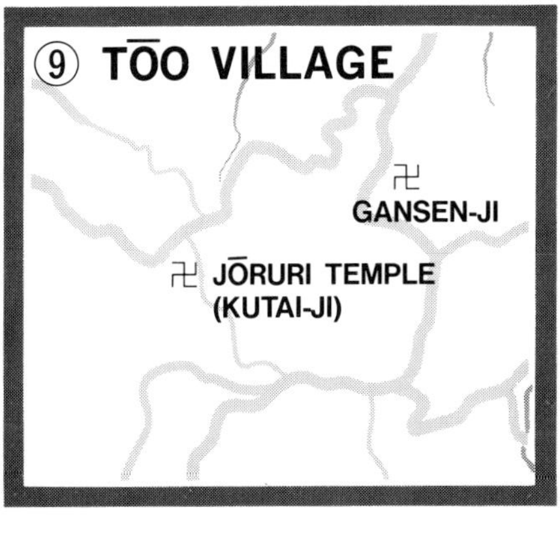

⑨ TŌO VILLAGE

卍 GANSEN-JI

卍 JŌRURI TEMPLE (KUTAI-JI)

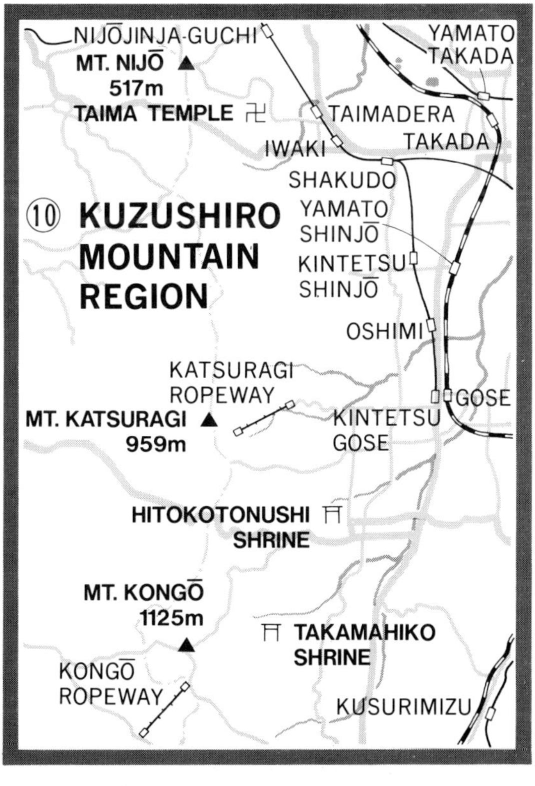

⑩ KUZUSHIRO MOUNTAIN REGION

NIJŌJINJA-GUCHI

MT. NIJŌ ▲ 517m

YAMATO TAKADA

TAIMA TEMPLE 卍

TAIMADERA

IWAKI

TAKADA

SHAKUDO

YAMATO SHINJŌ

KINTETSU SHINJŌ

OSHIMI

KATSURAGI ROPEWAY

MT. KATSURAGI ▲ 959m

GOSE

KINTETSU GOSE

HITOKOTONUSHI 鳥 SHRINE

MT. KONGŌ 1125m

▲

鳥 TAKAMAHIKO SHRINE

KONGŌ ROPEWAY

KUSURIMIZU

⑪ MT. YOSHINO

YAMATO
KAMIICHI
YOSHINO-
SHINGŪ

YOSHINO RIVER

YOSHINO
YOSHINOYAMA
KŌGAN-JI 卍   ZAŌ-DŌ
                卍
TŌNAN-IN 卍   卍 KATTE SHRINE
DAINICHI   卍 NYOIRIN-JI
TEMPLE   卍 CHIKURIN-IN

MT. YOSHINO

卍 MIKUMARI
   SHRINE

卍 KIMBU
   SHRINE

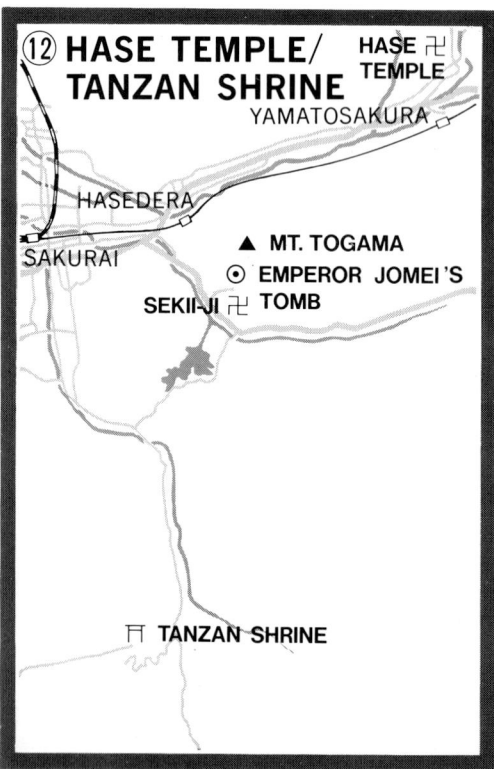

⑫ HASE TEMPLE/ TANZAN SHRINE

HASE 卍
TEMPLE

YAMATOSAKURA

HASEDERA

SAKURAI

▲ MT. TOGAMA

⊙ EMPEROR JOMEI'S
   TOMB

SEKII-JI 卍

卍 TANZAN SHRINE

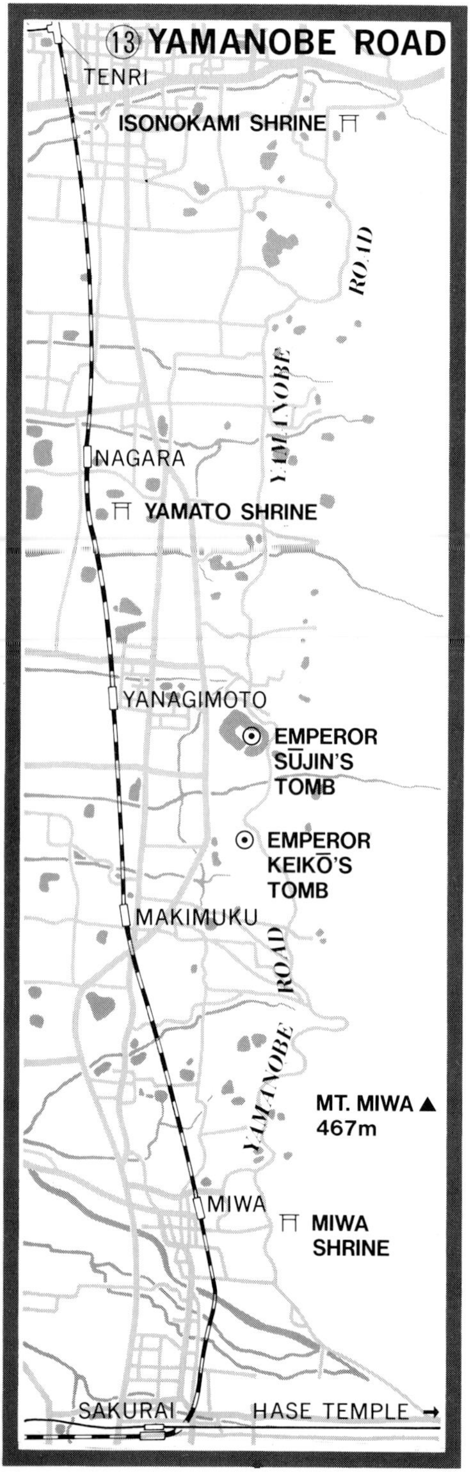

⑬ YAMANOBE ROAD

TENRI

ISONOKAMI SHRINE 卍

YAMANOBE ROAD

NAGARA

卍 YAMATO SHRINE

YANAGIMOTO

⊙ EMPEROR
   SŪJIN'S
   TOMB

⊙ EMPEROR
   KEIKŌ'S
   TOMB

MAKIMUKU

YAMANOBE ROAD

MT. MIWA ▲
467m

MIWA

卍 MIWA
   SHRINE

SAKURAI   HASE TEMPLE →

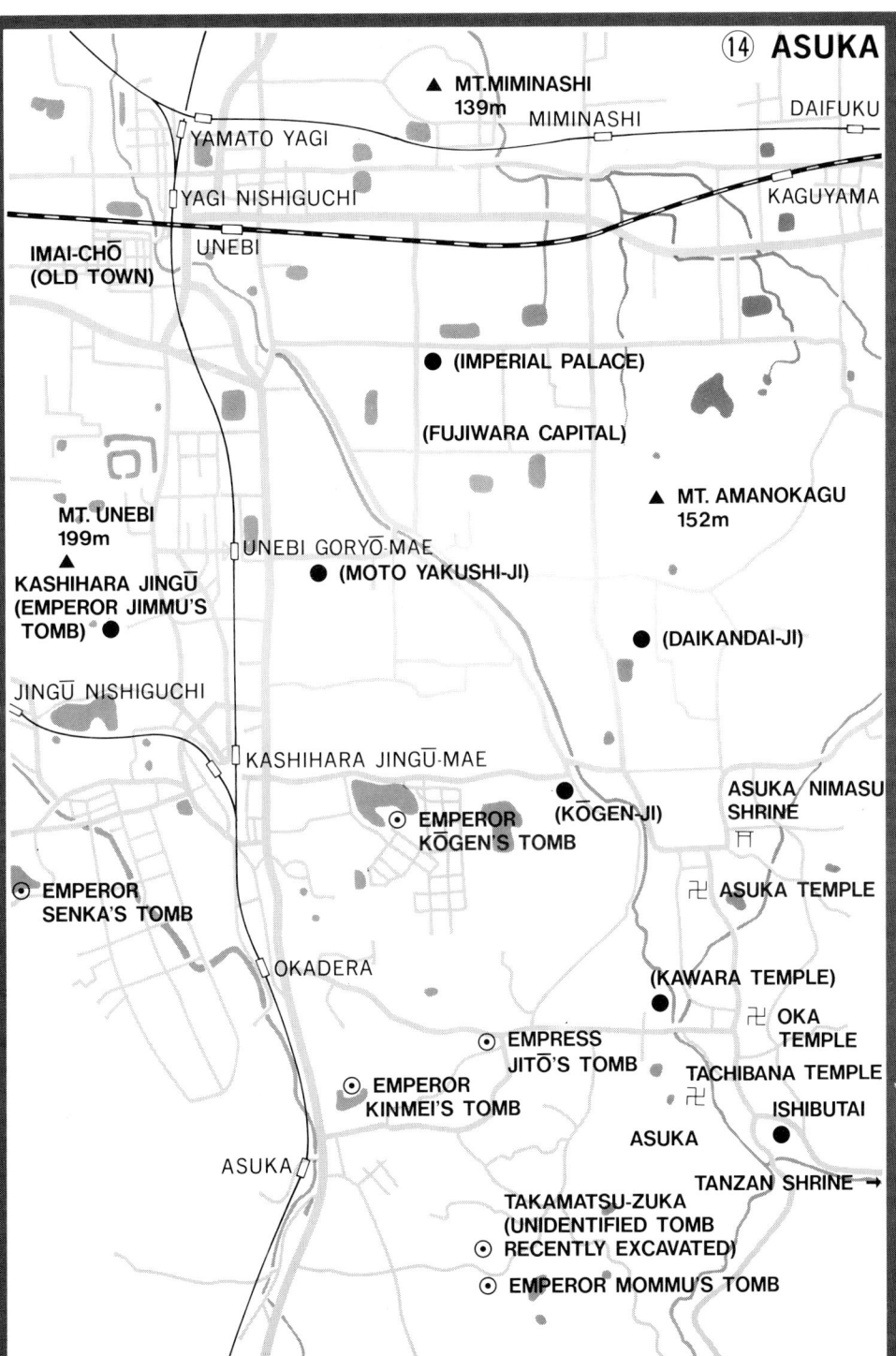

▲ MT.MIMINASHI
139m
MIMINASHI
DAIFUKU

YAMATO YAGI

YAGI NISHIGUCHI

KAGUYAMA

IMAI-CHŌ
(OLD TOWN)
UNEBI

● (IMPERIAL PALACE)

(FUJIWARA CAPITAL)

▲ MT. AMANOKAGU
152m

MT. UNEBI
199m
▲
KASHIHARA JINGŪ
(EMPEROR JIMMU'S
TOMB) ●

UNEBI GORYŌ-MAE
● (MOTO YAKUSHI-JI)

● (DAIKANDAI-JI)

JINGŪ NISHIGUCHI

KASHIHARA JINGŪ-MAE

● (KŌGEN-JI)

ASUKA NIMASU
SHRINE

⊙ EMPEROR
KŌGEN'S TOMB

卍 ASUKA TEMPLE

⊙ EMPEROR
SENKA'S TOMB

OKADERA

(KAWARA TEMPLE)
●

卍 OKA
TEMPLE

⊙ EMPRESS
JITŌ'S TOMB

TACHIBANA TEMPLE
卍

⊙ EMPEROR
KINMEI'S TOMB

ISHIBUTAI
●

ASUKA

ASUKA

TANZAN SHRINE →

TAKAMATSU-ZUKA
(UNIDENTIFIED TOMB
⊙ RECENTLY EXCAVATED)

⊙ EMPEROR MOMMU'S TOMB

BIBLIOGRAPHY OF QUOTED WORKS

Early Japanese History. By R.K. Reischauer (1967)

Kojiki. Transl. by B.H. Chamberlain (1932)

Kojiki. Transl. by D.L. Philippi (1968)

Manyōshū — One thousand poems —. Transl. by R. Hodgson (1940)

Miraculous Stories from the Japanese Buddhist Tradition —
     The Nihon ryōiki of the Monk Kyokai —. Tansl. by K. Motomochi Nakamura (1973)

Sources of Japanese History. Comp. by D.J. Lu (1974)

Sources of Japanese Tradition. Ed. by Wm. T. de Bary (1958)

INDEX